# Data Protection Codes of Practice

**NCC** Blackwell

MANCHESTER • OXFORD

British Library Cataloguing in Publication Data

Data protection codes of practice.

1. Computer systems. Data protection. Law

I. National Computing Centre

342.2'858

ISBN 0-85012-670-3

Published for NCC Publications by NCC Blackwell Limited.

Editorial Office: The National Computing Centre Limited, Oxford Road, Manchester M1 7ED, England.

NCC Blackwell Limited, 108 Cowley Road, Oxford OX4 1JF, England.

Typeset in 11pt Times Roman by Laser 27 Limited, Manchester; and printed by Hobbs the Printers of Southampton.

ISBN 0-85012-670-3

# Foreword

Data protection legislation is intended to dispel the widespread belief that computer held information is liable to misuse to the detriment of the person concerned. By laying down standards for the holding of personal data and by giving rights to the individual, the legislation seeks to ensure that data are only used in the approved way and are open to inspection by any person identified within the data.

The Data Protection Act came into effect in stages from 1985. It affects every concern that holds personal data and every computer bureau handling such data. The forty-three sections and four schedules of the Act must be considered within the general context of British law, as amended by Orders in Council. In addition, the Data Protection Registrar, who is the supervisory authority, publishes his understanding of the law in a variety of ways including Guidelines and, from time to time, guidance notes. At present (November 1989) the courts and tribunal have not been called upon to interpret the Act in particular cases. When they do, such interpretations should also be borne in mind.

These Codes of Practice have been developed with the intention of making compliance with the Data Protection Act simpler for users of information technology in specialised industries or carrying out specific tasks. They contain within a few pages the requirements of the legislation within the named areas. Therefore they should avoid any need to cross-reference the Act with the Guidelines, industry standards or interpretations from the courts. It is proposed that any material relevant to the legislation is read, especially the Guidelines issued by the Registrar, but that, for day-to-day administration, the relevant Code of Practice should be the only document necessary.

In some cases, the recommendations of the Codes of Practice go beyond what is strictly required by the law. This may be because the industry standards require it or simply because good practice or good relations with staff, customers or the public make the additional procedures desirable.

This volume is not intended to be read from end to end. Rather, each chapter shoud be read by those people using data in the specified way. For this reason sections of each code may be very similar. The repetition is necessary to allow each code to stand alone without reference to the others. Some parts of this volume will be relevant in every area; these are the conclusion, bibliography and appendix. Although each code carries a section on security requirements, these are dealt with more fully in the chapter on security and this is recommended reading for those wishing to know more details of appropriate security precautions.

The Codes of Practice have been developed by the NCC in co-operation with bodies representing users of data in the relevant trade, profession or industry. The names of the co-operating bodies are listed in the Acknowledgements. In addition each code has been checked by the Office of the Data Protection Registrar in fulfilment of the Registrar's obligation under section 36 of the Act to encourage the preparation of Codes of Practice. This has been a highly iterative process involving obtaining a consensus of the user bodies and NCC in each case, submitting the draft code to the Registrar, obtaining his opinion, amending the code as necessary and then resuming the cycle. Each code went through this process many times. Some codes have already received the endorsement of the Registrar, where approval is lacking this is due to lack of resources in the Registrar's Office.


Tony Elbra
Deputy Principal Consultant
Communication and Security Division

# Acknowledgements

NCC would like to acknowledge with thanks the support of the Department of Trade and Industry in the production of these Codes of Practice.

We would also like to thank the Data Protection Registrar and his Staff for their comments, advice and assistance in the preparation of these codes.

In addition thanks are due to the bodies listed below for their cooperation with the following chapters:

| | |
|---|---|
| Chapter One | BCS Computer Security Specialist Group |
| | BCS Data Protection Committee |
| | LAMSAC Data Protection Working Party |
| | NCC Data Protection Working Group |
| | NCC Security Circle |
| Chapter Two | Institute of Personnel Management |
| | Confederation of British Industry |
| | Industrial Society |
| Chapter Three | Computing Services Association |
| Chapter Four | Chartered Institute of Management Accountants |
| | Institute of Internal Auditors (UK) |
| | Institute of Purchasing and Supply |
| Chapter Five | Royal Pharmaceutical Society of Great Britain |
| Chapter Six | Incorporated Society of Valuers and Auctioneers |
| | National Association of Estate Agents |
| | Royal Institute of Chartered Surveyors. |

# Contents

# 1   IT Security

## Note by Data Protection Registrar

*I welcome this joint initiative by the Department of Trade and Industry and the NCC, in producing this guidance on security and the Data Protection Act 1984. Thanks are also due to the members of the groups who have provided input.*

*The Act requires computer users to take appropriate security measures in processing personal data. The guidance is helpful in highlighting the many matters which the user will need to take into account in developing his own particular circumstances, and it is therefore impossible in a general publication like this to specify detailed procedures and standards which would be appropriate to every user.*

*Experience in meeting the requirements of the Data Protection Act will develop over time, and it will be valuable to have comments from users on their experience in putting into effect appropriate security measures. I shall be happy to receive any comments of this nature.*

## 1.1 PURPOSE

This chapter explains what may be considered appropriate security measures within the Data Protection Act. It will enable the data user or computer bureau to interpret the Eighth Principle of that Act for their particular circumstances. It will also enable the data user to determine the security measures implicit in the other principles. It should be used by the responsible person in each organisation in order to develop the standards and procedures for that organisation.

## 1.2 INTRODUCTION

### 1.2.1 Security

Security is a wide subject, covering confidentiality, integrity and availability of data. Every data user and computer bureau should take steps to maintain the security of all the data under their control in their own interest. However, these notes address only the data covered by the Data Protection Act; ie personal data processed by or on behalf of a data user, possibly by a computer bureau.

The definitions of these terms are set out in section 1 of the Act, which should be consulted for clarification. The definitions are further explained in Guideline 2, issued by the Data Protection Registrar.

Briefly the Act applies to information stored in computer-readable form that relates to an identifiable living individual. This includes automatically retrieved microform and paper documents intended for OCR use. The Act is *not* restricted to data that may be considered 'sensitive'. The data user is the organisation that controls the use and content of the data while the data subject is the individual referred to in the data.

### 1.2.2 The Eighth Principle

There is an obligation on all data users to observe all the principles set out in Schedule 1 of the Act. There is an obligation on computer bureaux and data users alike to observe the Eighth Principle, viz:

> appropriate security measures shall be taken against unauthorised access to, or alteration, disclosure or destruction of personal data and against accidental loss or destruction of personal data.

This chapter is intended to explain what are appropriate security measures and to make it simpler for computer users of any sort to observe the Eighth Principle.

### 1.2.3  The Other Principles

Failure to provide adequate security may mean that other provisions of the Act cannot be met. In particular the Third and Fifth Principles may be breached.

Third Principle: Personal data held for any purpose or purposes shall not be used or disclosed in any manner incompatible with that purpose or those purposes.

Good security is necessary to ensure that the data are not being disclosed to unregistered persons or used in any way different from the registered purposes.

Fifth Principle: Personal data shall be accurate and, where necessary, kept up to date.

If unauthorised access to and alteration of data are permitted due to poor security provisions, there is no way of guaranteeing the accuracy of the data.

An explanation of all the principles is given in Guideline 4 issued by the Data Protection Registrar.

### 1.2.4  Sanctions

The prudent computer user will of course wish to provide appropriate security measures for his own benefit. Generally the requirements of the Act tie in closely with the aims of the computer user who will wish to keep data secure and accurate, to limit disclosure to the right people and to keep the data subject informed.

Nevertheless, the Act does provide for sanctions against those that choose to ignore its provisions. Failure to observe any of the principles may lead the Data Protection Registrar to issue an Enforcement Notice against the user or computer bureau. The Enforcement Notice will specify the nature of the breach and, in general terms, what must be done to correct matters. Failure to comply with an Enforcement Notice will be an offence and may lead to fines and deregistration.

## 1.3  WHAT SECURITY ENTAILS

### 1.3.1  Installation Requirements

For the computer installation, security means keeping correct data available at all times that the data are required. It therefore covers the prevention of loss or corruption of data, software, communications, equipment or confidentiality. The safety of the premises and the people working there are also included.

### 1.3.2  Data Protection Act Requirements

The Data Protection Act is concerned only with the rights of the individual. The security requirements in this context are limited to those that provide confidentiality of data, accuracy of data and the ability to satisfy the rights of access and correction. Confidentiality, integrity and availability are therefore all relevant. Within these broad descriptions, physical and logical access control, personnel procedures, development and maintenance of systems, general handling of data and information, contingency planning and audit are involved.

Under the Eighth Principle, measures are required against:

— unauthorised access (physical security, logical security);

— unauthorised alteration (logical security);

— unauthorised disclosure (physical security, logical security, personnel procedures, handling of data and information);

— unauthorised destruction (physical security, logical security, personnel procedures, handling of data and information);

— accidental loss (logical security, development and maintenance of systems);

— accidental destruction (contingency planning).

Under the Third Principle, disclosure of data must be restricted. This has implications for physical and logical security, personnel procedures and general handling of data and information. The Fifth Principle's requirements for accuracy means that consideration must be given to audit, logical security and development and maintenance of systems.

### 1.3.3   Commitment to Security

Security will depend above all else on the commitment of the management of the organisation. They must be seen to believe security to be important. Management should consider the risks inherent in their systems and set up controls and procedures to ensure that a high level of security is maintained. Security should regularly be reviewed with account taken of new techniques of data misuse and its prevention.

### 1.3.4   Security Criteria

In deciding whether or not a breach of the Eighth Principle is likely, the computer user should consider:

— if the measures taken are broadly in keeping with those taken by other organisations handling similar data;

— if the history of data usage in the installation shows that the security measures taken are adequate.

## 1.4   PHYSICAL SECURITY

### 1.4.1   Purpose of Physical Security

The purpose of this aspect of security is to preserve the computer equipment and its data from physical harm. From the data protection point of view the principal need is to restrict unauthorised access to the data. The safety from fire and other natural hazards, though important in its own right, can, as regards data protection, be adequately provided by contingency planning.

### 1.4.2   Physical Access Control

The degree of access control exercised must depend to some extent on the control applied to the building and the grounds as a whole. However, the control of access to the computer equipment is what is important, at whatever stage this is exercised.

The approach to mainframe computers should be controlled either by guards or by automatic means. Micro-computers and terminals should be placed in environments where access to them by unauthorised persons can plainly be seen. Any such unauthorised persons should be challenged. Security of such equipment can be improved by fitting a key, which will be removed when the equipment is not in use. Where terminals or micros are deliberately placed in public areas for public use, such equipment should be limited to access to publicly available data. (See Section 1.5 below.)

Physical access control through automatic means may be achieved by means of keys, card keys, combination locks, authentication calculators, radio transmitters, signature verification or any appropriate token. Some systems keep a record of entry into and egress from the restricted area. The issue of such tokens should be controlled so that, for example, keys are not left in the possession of ex-employees, combinations are changed at reasonable frequencies, etc. All tokens must be adequately protected when not in use. When designing physical access, consideration should be given to the number of times each approach will be used and the difficulty of using it as well as the need for security. The method to be used should be chosen accordingly.

Persons with the right of access to computer equipment must be easily recognised. A system of badges may be appropriate, but these should not double as a token for entrance by automatic means. Within a small organisation, permitted staff may be recognised by familiarity.

Care must also be exercised with regard to access to the media store, backing store, etc. The Act is intended to restrict access to data to those authorised, so all copies of the data and information derived therefrom must be adequately protected. With the increasing compactness of computer equipment and media there is the risk that micros, diskettes, magnetic tapes or other media may be removed. To prevent this, anything holding data should physically be secured in place or locked away when not in active use.

## 1.5  LOGICAL SECURITY

### 1.5.1  Purpose of Logical Security

Control of this type of security is intended to prevent end-users, whether authorised or not, from accessing or updating data beyond their authority. Also within logical security, steps should be taken to maintain the integrity of the data.

## 1.5.2   Logical Access Control

Control will depend on some identifying token similar to those used for physical access control, used singly or in combination. Such tokens must be properly controlled and steps must be taken to prevent their being lost or passed to the wrong people. Each token should be granted to one individual only so that in the event of its misuse one person is plainly responsible. If a physical token is lost, the person responsible for it should report its loss straightaway and recognition of that token should at once be withdrawn. Persons leaving the organisation or significantly changing their role should be required to hand back their tokens. Passwords or similar tokens based on knowledge rather than possession may be guessed by other people or they may be learned through their careless use. To guard against this, they should be changed frequently, the standard password supplied with the hardware or software should be disabled, easily guessed passwords should not be used and passwords should never be displayed. Details of valid tokens held on the computer should be encrypted.

For sensitive data it may be necessary to use more sophisticated access control procedures, such as passwords used only once, long passwords (of which only a part is used at one time) or multiple passwords for a single access.

## 1.5.3   Action Following Incorrect Access Attempt

When a person attempts to access or update data beyond his entitlement, this attempt should of course be frustrated. The action following this will depend on the sophistication of the hardware and software, on the sensitivity of the data and on the number of attempts made. For example, many installations permit a wrong password to be entered two or three times before refusing access. This allows for occasional mis-keying by genuine end-users.

Apart from refusing access, the following action may be taken:

— invite re-entry of the password;

— disable the terminal pending clarification;

— log the attempted misuse;

— immediate investigation by security staff.

Mainframe computer users should not permit an unlimited number of incorrect identifications to be made. A large number may indicate a hacker or fraudster trying every combination. Disablement of the terminal being misused is a reasonable action in these conditions. If a log is made of attempted violations, it should be selective to restrict its length and it should be inspected regularly. Any apparent violation should be investigated. A log will be useful to substantiate or deny any complaints made later by the data subject.

### 1.5.4  Integrity of Data

Every effort must be made to maintain data integrity. This can be aided by introducing control totals, section totals and batch controls, if appropriate, and checking these controls on a regular basis and after every major update.

### 1.5.5  Network Security

Data sent via telecommunications may be transmitted through private lines or public circuits. The latter should only be used if the authenticity of the receiving station can be established. This can be done through the use of identifying passwords at sign-on time or through dial-back routines always made to established addresses.

Private lines are safer but are still vulnerable to tapping. Computer users should consider whether or not their data are sufficiently sensitive or interesting or profitable to warrant this. The chief prevention against tapping is vigilance, eg looking out for bugs placed near the lines. If one is detected it should be removed and regular formal inspection instigated.

Hacking on public circuits is prevented by verifying every call made to the computer and calling back only recognised users. Encryption of data sent out via networks will ensure that any data incorrectly obtained will be incomprehensible to the eavesdropper. Encryption may also be used to authenticate the identity of the sender and receiver of messages. The history of violations or the perception of risk will largely determine the level at which these precautions should be set.

## 1.6  PERSONNEL

### 1.6.1  Obligations of the Data Protection Act

The Act specifies in the interpretation of the Eighth Principle that regard should be had:

> to the nature of the personal data and the harm that would result from such access, alteration, disclosure, loss or destruction as are mentioned in this principle;

and

> to the place where the personal data are stored, to security measures programmed into the relevant equipment and to measures taken for ensuring the reliability of staff having access to the data.

The reliability of staff will depend to a large extent on the security standards imposed by the management and the care taken with appointments.

The Act lays a requirement on data users and computer bureaux alike to observe the Eighth Principle and its interpretation. These requirements extend to the servants (employees) and agents of these bodies.

### 1.6.2  Training

All staff that handle data or information derived from data must be aware of the Act and the obligation that it imposes to use and disclose data only in accordance with the registered particulars.

Staff should also be aware of the importance of security as a means of safeguarding the interests of the installation and of preventing unauthorised disclosure or any mistreatment of the data.

To these ends the staff induction should include instruction on security and the implications of the Data Protection Act. Existing staff should be informed by notice or by attendance at training courses or by presentation of one or more of the commercially obtainable videos. The security and data protection procedures should be published in a form that is available to all relevant staff. Copies of the registered entries should also be made available to all staff. This will enable them more easily to identify cases where the registered particulars are likely to be exceeded.

In the event of a complaint of mishandling of data, the Registrar will take into account the steps taken to instruct staff and agents in their obligations as regards security.

### 1.6.3  Discipline

The management of any computer installation should be fully committed to security. Part of this commitment is to ensure that staff are equally committed. Any breaches of security should be followed up, even if they appear trivial. If small lapses in security are always investigated, the persons concerned and others will not be tempted to commit any greater misdemeanour.

The procedures should be practical, in that they will cause minimum inconvenience, but they should be strictly observed.

### 1.6.4  The Data Protection Co-ordinator

At least one member of staff should be given responsibility for data protection. Their function will be to keep abreast of developments, to liaise with the Registrar and to ensure that the data usage keeps in accordance with the register entries and with the principles. To allow for deputising, it may be necessary to appoint more than one person to this task. On the other hand, it is not always necessary to designate the co-ordinator as a full time function. It will combine readily with some other function such as database administrator or computer auditor.

### 1.6.5  Allocation of Tokens

Tokens needed for physical or logical access should be allocated with regard to the principles of 'need to know' and 'segregated duties'. The 'need to know' principle means that each individual should only be given access to data that he requires to know as part of his duties, and nothing else. By segregated duties is meant the arrangement that ensures that no one person is entirely in charge of any one function. For example, the person that places an order should not be the same person as the one that raises the cheque in payment. This principle makes it difficult to carry out a fraud unless there is collusion between two individuals carrying out separate functions. Tokens must be allocated on an individual basis rather than a divisional or functional basis, so that misuse is easily traced to the responsible persons.

## 1.7  DEVELOPMENT AND MAINTENANCE OF SYSTEMS

### 1.7.1  Importance

However much care is taken of the data, it will be of no avail if the systems handling the data are allowed to become corrupt. Then the systems will allow possible loss of the data or unauthorised alteration. These are of course contrary to the Eighth Principle. Loss of data is also one of the circumstances that will allow a data subject to claim damages, if any are suffered thereby.

### 1.7.2  Development of Systems

It is important that systems are developed in accordance with the requirements of the organisation. Therefore any new system should be fully specified in advance and agreed before live work is allowed to commence. This will suppose comprehensive testing to the satisfaction of the end-user and a formal signing-off from the end-user and audit that the system appears satisfactory.

Live data about actual individuals should not be used as part of test data unless the data user is prepared to observe the Data Protection Act with regard to those data. This means taking as much care over the security and accuracy of the test data as with live data and being ready to grant subject access to the test data if required. For practical reasons, this use of data is not recommended. If test data contain fictitious information apparently about real people, this fact should be plainly indicated.

### 1.7.3  Maintenance of Systems

Any required maintenance should be fully specified in advance and thoroughly tested and agreed before live use. Documentation should show the changes made and the reasons for them. An exception must be made for urgent changes made overnight or at holiday times in order to keep operational systems running. These will not be specified in advance; nevertheless they should be properly tested and information as to the changes done should be left for subsequent investigation, approval and documentation. Change control procedures along these lines should be introduced and applied independently of end-users and system development teams.

### 1.7.4  Use of Libraries

A distinction should be made between software held for operational use and that undergoing testing and not yet proved. The two types should be differentiated by being held on distinct libraries, an operational library for working software and a development library for software under test. Programming staff should never have access to the operational library, whereas the development library should never be used operationally. Moving a program in any form to the operational library should only be done with a formal and signed permission to do so.

## 1.8  HANDLING OF DATA AND INFORMATION

### 1.8.1  Care of Media

Data may be destroyed if the media containing them are not handled correctly. All staff having anything to do with magnetic tapes or disks, diskettes or cassettes should be informed of the proper way to keep and handle them. This applies among other things to media sent elsewhere by courier or through the post. These should be properly protected from rough treatment and the weather. Tapes should be in specially designed padded containers and diskettes should be enclosed in padded holders. Hard disks should not be transported at all except under the personal care of a responsible individual. Any data transported outside the installation should first be copied on to media to be kept at the installation. Transported data should be sealed to avoid illicit copying in transit.

Data should only be transported where the intended recipient is registered as a disclosee of the appropriate data. Only trustworthy carriers and data storers should be used; they will be acting as the agents of the data user and need not be registered as disclosees.

Personal data must be removed from any media before the media are sold or sent for destruction.

### 1.8.2  Personal Data Used Elsewhere

Procedures should be laid down for personnel carrying data in any form outside the premises of the computer user. They should take care of these data to prevent any unauthorised disclosure taking place. If members of staff wish to take data to use on their home computer, procedures should be laid down for this too. These should specify that the home computer must only be used as specified within the registered purposes and that reasonable security precautions must continue to be taken. Data used elsewhere are still covered by the Act and must be available for data subject access if requested. Sensitive personal data should not be used in this way at all.

### 1.8.3 Use of Hardware by End-users

The registration made should reflect the use by the organisation of data of all sorts, whether held on mainframe or micros. There is a danger that end-users may develop an independent frame of mind and seek to initiate their own systems without any consultation with the Data Protection Co-ordinator. This misdeed is made easier if they are allowed to purchase their own micros without consultation. As a result they may develop unregistered applications that incidentally contravene many of the principles due to the poor level of security provided. To guard against this, all computer hardware and software should be centrally obtained and used only for the permitted purposes. This is not to say that end-users should not develop their own systems, only that their intentions should be known in advance and that their standards should conform to those of the rest of the organisation.

Micro security capabilities are generally less than those obtainable with mainframes. However security can be improved by the use of hardware and software packages designed to limit access and sometimes to provide encryption. Access can be obtained to mainframes from micros: this should be subject to the same controls as access from a terminal.

### 1.8.4 Disclosure

Although the Act is primarily concerned with personal data, there is one area where it extends to the information that may constitute the data. This is the area of disclosure. Section 1 (7) states that:

'Disclosing', in relation to data, includes disclosing information extracted from the data . . .

It follows from this that care must be taken with hard copy and with screen displays. Unauthorised access to such information must be prevented and any disclosure must be within the registered particulars.

This obligation, subject to the exemptions specified in the Act, extends to the life of the material which may exceed the life of the data.

People handling personal data should be aware of the risk of improper disclosure and should be warned against passing on any personal information to unauthorised individuals. Generally this means persons whose duties do not require knowledge of the particular piece of information. Staff should avoid passing information to unidentified people, including those claiming to be data subjects, particularly over the telephone. Staff should not discuss personal information gleaned from work, with people outside work, however interesting. The contract of employment or the staff notice issued in explanation of the Act should make this clear.

Personal information held on input forms should also be kept securely.

### 1.8.5 Screen Display

Information displayed on a VDU may be observed by the wrong people unless proper care is taken. To prevent unauthorised disclosure, screens displaying personal data should be positioned so that they cannot be viewed by people other than those intended. They should not face outside windows where these may be overlooked and they should not face public areas. Sometimes the intention may be that the public should have access for the purpose of viewing their own data. In that case the logical access controls must be such that each individual is permitted to see his own data only and update by an outsider is prevented.

Screens should not be left on, unattended; especially while displaying personal information. If an operator wishes to leave a terminal, he should log off or at least remove any personal information from the screen.

Electronic eavesdropping involves setting up directional aerials and picking up the radiation emitted from VDUs or other equipment, sometimes at considerable distances. The radiation collected may be displayed on a pirate screen in exactly the same form as the original display, or it may be recorded for later, more leisurely interrogation. Some organisations will feel that their data is vulnerable to this threat, because knowledge of their data would be useful to a rival concern. Such organisations should carry out a proper assessment of the risks before deciding on action in response to this threat.

### 1.8.6  Hard Copy

Computer print-outs and microform output are more liable to misuse than data displayed on a screen because their life is much longer. Such information can survive for many years and is unlikely to attract the same level of security precautions all through its life.

Staff must be informed of the need to take care with output obtained from personal data. This care should extend to not using or leaving it in places where it may be overlooked. The practice of using old computer print-outs as scrap paper or as drawing material for one's infants should not be allowed where personal data has been involved.

The practice of leaving print-outs on a desktop overnight should be discouraged. Prints should be put away in locked cabinets when not in use. Sufficient lockable cabinets must be provided for this purpose.

When the useful life of computer output has come to an end, steps should be taken for its safe destruction. This sounds paradoxical, but it means that it should be destroyed under conditions where it is unlikely that the information contained will be seen by unauthorised persons. Shredding of paper may be one way of achieving safe destruction, but is probably too laborious for large volumes. Shredding is insufficiently fine for microform output. Pulping under supervision is another way. Many organisations sell their outdated print-outs to scrap paper merchants who will then arrange pulping. Provided that reasonable care is taken with the scrap paper this practice should be allowed to continue. Most scrap paper merchants handling computer print-out will give a written indemnity against loss of confidentiality. Nevertheless it is the responsibility of the data user to satisfy himself that proper precautions are taken.

Similar precautions should be taken with carbon paper and printer ribbons, especially those used only once.

## 1.9  CONTINGENCY PLANNING

### 1.9.1  Significance

Prudent computer users will wish to take all reasonable steps to ensure security but will realise that mishaps can still occur. They will wish to ensure that their computing capability suffers only the minimum disruption following one of these mishaps. Contingency planning is the technique of planning for the unexpected and of ensuring that at least the essential work can continue. As organisations become more dependent on their computers, contingency planning can make all the difference between survival and failure. Because of their importance all contingency plans should be tested from time to time, particularly following changes in hardware or software.

### 1.9.2   Care of Media and Documentation

Care must be taken with the media and the data, software and documentation that they contain. The media should be accommodated in storage specifically designed for the purpose and not left casually in drawers or on desk tops, etc. Sufficient back-up copies must be taken to ensure that, in the event of an accident, the data may be re-created in its previous form. To ensure that the back-up will be available after a fire, they should be held in fireproof storage. As an additional precaution, some of the copies should be held at a site remote from the computer installation. The remote copies are unlikely to be engulfed by the same disaster that sweeps away the computer installation and so should be instantly available after the event.

### 1.9.3   Insurance

Sufficient insurance should be taken out to cover the increased cost of working when using a standby computer installation.

### 1.10   AUDIT

### 1.10.1   Purpose

As far as data protection is concerned, the purpose of audit should be to advise on the effectiveness of control systems and to minimise the possible cost caused by legal action or the imposition of fines or deregistration. The auditor should therefore interest himself in compliance with the Act and in following this and other appropriate Guidelines and Codes of Practice.

### 1.10.2   Functions of Audit

The internal auditor should take steps to monitor compliance with the data protection principles. To this end he should become familiar with the registered purposes and ensure that proposed systems or changes to systems do not go beyond them. A good method of documentation would be a help.

The auditor should become involved with system design at an early stage so that the system would incorporate good audit practices from the beginning. These would include such features as control accounts and an audit trail. The internal auditor should be aware of possible fraudulent practices, such as corruption of files and programs and be watchful for fraud where there is a risk. The control figures should be subject to frequent checks and should be designed to make falsification as difficult as possible.

The internal auditor should keep an eye on logs of illegal access (physical or logical) and be watchful for any unusual circumstances or breaches of security. Checks should be made at random intervals and any unusual happening should be investigated. The auditor should make sure that security is kept to a high level throughout the organisation. Security is everyone's concern but should interest the auditor, the line manager and the computer manager in particular.

The function of the external auditor is to act on behalf of shareholders, ratepayers or other concerned parties. In their interests the external auditor should also check that the law on data protection is followed.

## 1.11  CHECKLIST

### Physical Security
  Restricted areas
  Guards
  Automatic control
  Control of tokens
  Badges

### Logical Security
  Control of tokens
  Action following misuse
  Logs of attempted misuse
  Control figures
  Precautions against hacking and tapping
  Private lines
  Encryption

Special password techniques

**Personnel**
Care with appointments
Training in security
Knowledge of procedures
Registered entries available
Reminders of Data Protection Act
Data Protection Co-ordinator
Need to know
Segregated duties
Tokens allocated individually

**Development and Maintenance of Systems**
Full specification
Full testing
Formal acceptance
No live data used in testing
Change control procedures
Test and operational libraries
Reversion copies of software

**Handling of Data and Information**
Transport of data
Registration of recipient
Home computer use
Registration of micro-held data
Passing on of information
Identity of enquirers
Contract of employment
Siting of screens
Leaving screens unattended
Electronic eavesdropping
Keeping print and microform
Destruction of print and microform

**Contingency Planning**
Fully tested plan
Regular review
Back-up
Remote back-up

**Audit**
Check on registered purposes
Involvement with system design
Check on logs

# 2   Code of Practice for Employee Data

***Note by Data Protection Registrar***

*I welcome the development of this code. It is a valuable initiative by the Institute of Personnel Management and the National Computing Centre. I am pleased to note that it was produced in collaboration with the Confederation of British Industry and the Industrial Society.*

*The code will give useful guidance to those using personal data for personnel administration — a sensitive and complex area — as to the practices which will assist them to comply with the data protection principles. In particular, I believe the emphasis given to the practical application of the principles in this code will prove particularly helpful to data users.*

*As Registrar, I have a duty to promote the observance of the data protection principles and to consider any complaints that they may have been breached. Observance of this code does not constitute an assurance that I will accept in all cases and without qualification that data users have complied with the Act. However, in considering relevant complaints it is my intention to give careful regard to whether the data user concerned has been complying with this code and will take such compliance as a positive factor in his or her favour.*

*I am sure that we will continue to learn by experience so it is pleasing to see that the Institute intends to monitor experience of the code. This will help to ensure that the standards of good practice it promotes* can be maintained and indeed enhanced. I hope to be able to co-operate with them in the process.

I now look to data users to develop their own more detailed procedures which will ensure that the data protection principles are met and that this code is put fully into operation.

## 2.1 INTRODUCTION

### 2.1.1 Purpose

The Data Protection Act gives rights to employees, as well as other individuals, about whom information is automatically processed. These rights are the right of access to personal information held on computers, the right to compensation for inaccuracy or loss of data, and the right to correction or erasure of inaccurate data. The Act places obligations on employers who hold data about employees and other individuals. They must, unless covered by one of the limited exemptions, register certain details defined by the Act, allow individuals access to data about themselves, and comply with the data protection principles laid down in Schedule 1 of the Act.

This code is intended to give practical assistance to personnel administrators and others handling employee data in complying with the Act. It is designed to help data users and computer bureaux to interpret the principles of the Act for their particular circumstances. The code should be read in conjunction with the guidelines and further information issued by the Data Protection Registrar and in the light of judgements by the Courts.

The use of data for personnel purposes will normally be covered by two of the standard purposes defined by the Data Protection Registrar for registration purposes as follows:

P001 The administration of prospective, current and past employees, including, where applicable, self employed or contract personnel, secondees, temporary staff or voluntary workers.

P002 The planning and management of the data user's workload or business activity.

### 2.1.2 Scope

This code refers to data covered by the Data Protection Act, ie personal data recorded in a form in which they can be processed by equipment operating automatically, as defined in the Act, by or on behalf of a data user.

The definitions of the above terms are set out in section 1 of the Act, which should be consulted for clarification. Briefly, the Act is concerned only with computer-held data which relate to a living individual. The data subject is the individual to whom the data relate.

The data user is the organisation that controls the use and content of the data, whether it processes the data on its own equipment or makes use of another's processing facilities, ie a computer bureau. The term computer bureau refers to a person or organisation which provides data services to others, either by processing data for others by equipment operating automatically, as defined in the Act, or by allowing others to use equipment in its possession to carry out such processing. This might apply, for example, where payroll or records data are administered by a third-party on a contract basis. A full definition is contained in the Act.

This code is intended to assist employers who are data users in complying with the Act. It is a statement of good personnel practice with the aim of promoting high standards.

### 2.1.3 Sanctions

Generally the requirements of the Act reflect the aims of the good computer user who will wish to keep data secure and accurate, to limit disclosure to the right people and to keep the data subject informed. However, failure by a data user to observe any of the principles (or in in the case of a computer bureau, the Eighth Principle) may lead the Data Protection Registrar to issue an Enforcement Notice requiring compliance. The Enforcement Notice will specify the nature of the breach and, in general terms, what must be done to correct matters. Failure to comply with an Enforcement Notice will be an offence and may lead to fines. The Registrar also has the power to deregister a data user by using a Deregistration Notice. Such a notice can be issued after failure to comply with an Enforcement Notice or when the nature of the case merits it. A data user who continued to process personal data covered by the Deregistration Notice would be committing a criminal offence.

### 2.1.4 Structure

Each data protection principle is quoted below and considered with particular reference to its applicability to personnel matters.

There is an obligation on all data users to observe all the principles;

and in addition, an obligation on computer bureaux to observe the Eighth Principle.

## 2.2  THE FIRST PRINCIPLE

The information to be contained in personal data shall be obtained, and personal data shall be processed, fairly and lawfully.

### 2.2.1  Interpretation

Anyone providing information should not be deceived or misled as to the purposes for which the data will be used or disclosed. Information is always treated as having been fairly obtained when the person from whom the information was obtained was authorised or required by law to supply it.

Similarly, information disclosed by a person will always be treated as having been fairly obtained to the extent that the disclosure was required and authorised by law, even though the disclosure may not have been indicated to the data subject at the time the information was collected, eg information provided to the DSS when required or authorised by statute will be fairly obtained.

'Processing' is defined by the Act to mean amending, adding to, deleting or rearranging the data or extracting the information that forms the data. Fairness in respect of obtaining and processing information will need to be judged by reference to the purposes of the data user and the consequences for the data subject.

Data held for historical, statistical or research purposes and not used in a way likely to cause damage or distress will not be regarded as having been obtained unfairly merely because these uses were not specified to the person providing the information.

### 2.2.2  Fair Collection and Use of Data

Employees or potential employees should not be induced to provide information or be led to believe that a failure to supply information might disadvantage them where this cannot be justified by the needs of personnel administration. Personnel administrators should be aware that they may be required to justify the collection of items of data.

Data collected for the purpose of personnel administration should be obtained from reliable sources which are included in the registration details and should be used only for this purpose. Following the Registrar's guidance on registration, the following are typical uses of personnel data which might reasonably be expected:

— recruitment;

— recording of working time;

— administration and payment of wages, salaries, pensions and other benefits, including deductions;

— employee assessment and training;

— negotiation or communication with employees;

— manpower and career planning;

— compliance with policy and/or legislation with regard to health, safety or other employment matters;

— job or task scheduling;

— roster administration;

— progress of piecework monitoring;

— identification of relevant resources;

— monitoring the use or performance of plant, equipment, vehicles or services;

— analysis for management purposes and statutory returns;

— provision of references.

### 2.2.3 Recommendations

Personnel administrators should:

— not use data held about employees for other activities such as marketing or selling, without the knowledge and consent of the employee(s) concerned;

— adopt a clear policy on personnel data and communicate this to all employees and prospective employees. They may wish to consider adding a statement on application and other relevant forms to the effect that the information collected will be strictly confidential and used only for the purposes of personnel administration.

If any other purpose is intended, this should be stated at the time the data are collected;

— only collect personal information that is required for legitimate business or legal reasons;

— ensure that the organisation's employees are aware of its data protection policies and are held accountable for complying with them.

## 2.3  THE SECOND PRINCIPLE

Personal data shall be held only for one or more specified and lawful purposes.

### 2.3.1  Interpretation

This principle is complied with provided that the data user processes data only in accordance with the purpose(s) registered.

### 2.3.2  Exemptions

Data held but exempt from the provisions of Part II of the Act need not be registered. For personnel administration, the Act provides a narrowly defined exemption for payroll processing only.

### 2.3.3  Recommendations

— Personnel administrators should register under Standard Purpose P001. They should also consider whether they may need to register under any other purpose, such as P002.

— It is advised that the payroll exemption should not be used due to its narrow scope and payroll data should be registered in the same way as other personnel data for the purposes of the Act.

— Personnel administrators must ensure that all processing of data about employees conforms to the registered particulars. This includes any independent processing of data about employees by individual managers, eg on personal computers.

— Personnel administrators should ensure that registered particulars are kept up to date and are amended or renewed as appropriate.

## 2.4  THE THIRD PRINCIPLE

Personal data held for any purpose or purposes shall not be used or disclosed in any manner incompatible with that purpose or those purposes.

### 2.4.1  Interpretation

This principle will be complied with provided that data are used or disclosed only in accordance with the registered details.

### 2.4.2  Exemptions

In certain circumstances, data may be disclosed even though the disclosure has not been registered. For example, data may always be disclosed:

— to an agent authorised by the employee who is the subject of the data;

— to an agent of the employer acting in his capacity as such. Care should be taken to distinguish between an agent, eg solicitors acting for a company, and an independent contractor, eg builder. The latter would not be entitled to rely on an exemption;

— to a member of staff acting within his duties;

— when required by statute, by any rule of law or by order of the court;

— for purposes of law enforcement and if urgently required for the prevention of injury and damage to health. Where a disclosure is made for law enforcement purposes, ie for the prevention or detection of crime, the apprehension or prosecution of offenders, or the assessment or collection of any tax or duty, the disclosure is exempt only where not to make the disclosure would be likely to prejudice one of those purposes;

— with the consent of the employee concerned. Employers need not register copious disclosures about employees, but may instead rely upon the option to disclose with employee consent.

An employer who relies properly on these exemptions does not commit a criminal offence by making a disclosure even though he is not registered to do so, nor does the disclosure amount to a breach of any of the data protection principles.

Care should be taken when relying on any of the above exemptions and particular care should be taken if relying on the exemption for a law enforcement purpose. In this situation an employer can rely on the exemption only if he is able to show that not to have made a disclosure would have been likely to prejudice such a law enforcement purpose. When seeking to use this exemption, an employer would be advised to obtain appropriate written evidence from the police, Inland Revenue or Customs and Excise that the request for disclosure meets the criteria set out in the Act.

### 2.4.3 Recommendations

— Data should be used or disclosed only in accordance with registered details, unless one of the exemptions is relied on, and subject to the data protection principles.

— To ensure compliance with the Act and in the interests of privacy, employee confidence and good employee relations, personnel administrators should seek to restrict the range of disclosures which are made without obtaining employee consent. With due regard to the resources available to a given organisation, personnel administrators should endeavour to restrict disclosures outside the organisation to those required by law. They should seek, wherever possible, to obtain an employee's written consent, even if the disclosure in question has been registered. Alternatively employers should advise employees of likely disclosures at the time the data are collected.

Having determined the appropriate policy to follow, the employer must ensure that only disclosures authorised under that policy are made. This last consideration is necessary to secure compliance with the Eighth Data Protection Principle. In short, employers must ensure not only that a disclosure is registered but also that it is authorised under the policy of the organisation.

In meeting these obligations, personnel administrators should be satisfied about the legitimacy of requests for information and seek valid documentary evidence where appropriate.

It is good personnel practice to define clearly the internal restrictions on access to personal data in order to enhance confidentiality. Personnel administrators should have a clear policy to ensure that data about employees can be accessed only where there is a legitimate 'business need to know', for example, to obtain details of an employee in respect of work being carried out by that employee for his manager. Again, having established a policy on internal access to data, employers should see that this is followed by employees to ensure compliance with the requirement in the Eighth Principle that only authorised access, ie that provided by company policy, is given.

## 2.5 THE FOURTH PRINCIPLE

Personal data held for any purpose or purposes shall be adequate, relevant and not excessive in relation to that purpose or those purposes.

### 2.5.1 Interpretation

No formal interpretation of this principle is provided in the Act.

### 2.5.2 Adequacy and Relevance

Whether or not information is adequate, relevant and not excessive will depend on the circumstances of a particular case. Personnel and administrators should therefore consider carefully whether the amount and nature of the information they gather about individuals is sufficient, relevant and not excessive for the purpose of personnel administration.

Personnel data may include personal details, job details, details of payments, benefits, training, qualifications, disciplinary matters, assessments of performance etc. For such data to be adequate and relevant, they should seek to provide sufficient but not excessive information, all of which will be, or is likely to be, used for manpower decisions. Computerised data may also be supplemented by manual information, and this will be pertinent to any assessment of the adequacy and relevance of the data. Where data are not kept up to date, they may well become inadequate. Where they are kept for longer than necessary, they may be both irrelevant and excessive. For example, details of qualifications used as a basis for promotion would clearly be inadequate if they were not kept up to date.

### 2.5.3 Recommendation

— Personnel administrators should consider the data which are held in the light of the full range of their activities. They should seek to identify the minimum amount of information about each individual which is required to fulfil their purposes. They should be aware that they may be required to provide an explanation as to why items of data are being held. Information which cannot be reasonably justified should not be gathered.

## 2.6  THE FIFTH PRINCIPLE

Personal data shall be accurate and, where necessary, kept up to date.

### 2.6.1  Interpretation

Data are considered inaccurate for the purpose of this principle if they are incorrect or misleading as to any matter of fact. An opinion, which is not a statement of fact, cannot be challenged on grounds of inaccuracy.

### 2.6.2  Updating

Updating is required only 'where necessary', so data held as a record of past transactions are unlikely to be in need of updating although they should have been accurate at the time they were collected. Where, however, data are used to make current judgements about individuals, there is clearly a need for accurate and up-to-date information.

### 2.6.3  Steps to Ensure Accuracy

A number of steps are available to help to ensure the accuracy of data, including:

— reasonable checks on the accuracy of data provided by reference to original documentation or to third parties;

— checks built into the software to help ensure that data are validated on entry and comply with certain predetermined criteria, for example, that a salary falls between the minimum and maximum for a given grade;

— procedures to ensure that any changes to software are properly validated and approved;

— investigation of the cause of any errors detected and correction of the faulty data, software or procedures, as appropriate;

— the periodical provision to employees of a copy of their record with an opportunity to raise queries, investigate them and correct the record where appropriate without prejudice to any rights which they have under the Act.

In addition, to provide a defence against claims by employees, it may be possible to add a 'marker' in each data field to denote whether data were received from an employee or a third party, and whether the data are disputed by the employee. The marker and the fact that data are disputed should also appear on any information extracted from the data. The use of such markers in compliance with the Act is complex and may not be considered practicable by data users.

### 2.6.4  Recommendations

Personnel administrators should:

— seek to verify information provided by reference to documentary evidence, wherever appropriate;

— take reasonable steps to ensure accuracy by providing employees with copies of relevant, current data to be checked for accuracy, possibly at annual intervals. Any errors should of course be removed;

— take steps to encourage employees to notify changes in their current circumstances and to ensure that they know the procedure to follow. Induction courses, employee handbooks, briefing sessions, and notices to employees are some of the ways by which this can be achieved. Where changes of circumstances are notified, the data should be changed accordingly as soon as is practicable. The urgency of this will clearly be dependent on the sensitivity of the information and the likely consequences of its being inaccurate.

### 2.7  THE SIXTH PRINCIPLE

Personal data held for any purpose or purposes shall not be kept for longer than is necessary for that purpose or those purposes.

### 2.7.1  Interpretation

Data held for historical, statistical or research purposes may be held indefinitely provided that the data are used in such a way that no damage or distress is, or is likely to be, caused to any data subject.

### 2.7.2  Present and Past Employees

An important reason for holding data about present or past employees is to meet subsequent legal or statutory claims. The time periods involved vary from a few months to many years, according to the limitation period provided for in a given statute. In the case of industrial diseases, for example, this may involve keeping data for twenty or thirty years or even longer. Data may also be held for analysing manpower trends and responding to requests for references. Data held only for statistical or research purposes, which are not used in a way likely to cause damage or distress, may be held indefinitely.

Where statutory limitation periods apply, as in the case of data relating to health and safety, payments and deductions, pensions fund records, redundancy and unfair dismissal, these provide guidance on the minimum periods for holding certain data. Where they do not, as in the case of most personal data, judgements will need to be made about how long data should be held for analytical or reference purposes.

### 2.7.3  Prospective Employees

Information about prospective employees may be held as a database of possible future recruits, and data about applicants may be held for the purpose of equal opportunities monitoring. Where current decisions are to be made on the basis of information provided in the past, as in the case of data on potential recruits, the individuals concerned should be notified what data are being held and should be given an opportunity to update the information. Such information should not be kept longer than necessary. It should not be kept, for example, if it is unlikely to be used for recruitment purposes in the foreseeable future.

### 2.7.4  Recommendations

— Personnel administrators should develop, in consultation with internal and external auditors, a policy on how long and in what detail records will be held to meet statutory claims or legitimate business needs. The policy should be regularly reviewed.

— Deletions should be carried out at appropriate intervals to remove data that are no longer required.

— In cases where there is no legal requirement to delete personal data, eg where data are held for historical, statistical or research purposes, personnel administrators are encouraged to depersonalise such data held, where this is practical, to prevent identification of a particular individual.

## 2.8  THE SEVENTH PRINCIPLE

An individual shall be entitled:

(a)  at reasonable intervals and without undue delay or expense:

   i) to be informed by any data user whether he holds personal data of which that individual is the subject; and

   ii) to access to any such data.

(b)  where appropriate, to have such data corrected or erased.

### 2.8.1  Interpretation

The principle should be interpreted by reference to section 21 of the Act which sets out the rights of subject access in more detail. 'Reasonable' intervals between access requests will be interpreted in the light of the nature of the data, their purpose and the frequency with which they are updated. The correction or erasure of data is appropriate only where necessary to comply with other data protection principles.

### 2.8.2  Data to be Provided

All data, current and historical, held on an individual employee, including both facts and opinions, such as assessments of current performance and future potential, fall within the definition of personal data. Data coming under the overall description of personnel information may be held on more than one system within the organisation and may also include, for example, employee data held by line managers on personal computers.

Access need not be provided to what the Act terms the 'intentions' of the data user. Intentions may include specific promotion plans, planned salary increases or other intentions of the organisation in relation to the employee, such as redundancy, early retirement, secondment or redeployment.

Where data to which access is being provided contains a reference identifying another individual, the data need not be disclosed unless the other individual has consented to the disclosure. However, the data should still give as much information as possible to the data subject without revealing the identity of the other individual. This may involve editing the material to remove names or other identifying features.

Data held only for statistical purposes or research are exempt from the subject access provisions on the condition that the resulting statistics or the results of the research do not identify individuals, and that the data are not used or disclosed for any other purpose. If it is impractical to depersonalise the data then personnel administrators should establish policies to ensure that the identities are not revealed.

### 2.8.3 Requests in Writing

Data users are obliged to respond only to requests made in writing, and are entitled to request reasonable further information to help locate the required records, for example, in the case of former employees. The data user is also entitled to charge a fee for the request, subject to a statutory maximum. The current maximum fee (November 1989) is £10. Employers need to decide whether to charge the full fee, a reduced fee or no fee at all. To facilitate the request process, personnel administrators may wish to develop a standard form for such requests, although they must respond to all requests, however presented. They may also wish to maintain records of the subject access requests received and dealt with.

### 2.8.4 Response

Once a request has been received, the data user is obliged to reply within 40 days. The period does not commence until the data user has received all the information reasonably required to identify the individual requiring access and to locate the data. During the time between receiving the request and replying to it, any normal amendments, insertions or deletions may be made to the individual's data, for example, a salary increase. However, no special changes should be made simply because the request has been received.

The data should be provided to the individual in written form and should be intelligible, with any coded information fully explained.

### 2.8.5  Identification of the Enquirer

In order to prevent inadvertent disclosure to an unauthorised person, the identity of the enquirer should be established. For an employee, this can usually be done through visual recognition. If identity cannot be proved by these means, it may be established by presentation of a payslip or other restricted document, by quoting a payroll number, a National Insurance number, or by giving a checkable signature.

The evidence of identity that employers might reasonably require will, of course, depend on particular circumstances. For example, where a reply is to be sent to an address known to be that of the employee or former employee then this would be reasonable proof of identity. If possible the established home address should always be used for those employees absent because of illness or other reason.

### 2.8.6  Location of Data Required

To establish the data required, the enquirer should be asked to quote an appropriate employee number, pay point or pay office, department, branch etc, dependent on the size and nature of the organisation.

Employees should be asked for any additional information which may help to identify the data in which they are interested. This will help to locate obscure records which may be registered separately from the main personnel files, particularly on micros and personal computers.

### 2.8.7  Exemptions

Exemptions from subject access apply to data held for various purposes. Of particular relevance to personnel administrators is the payroll data exemption, which is a conditional exemption not only from the subject access provisions, but also from the whole of the Act. This is a narrowly defined exemption. Where it does apply, employers may nevertheless wish to treat payroll data in the same way as personnel data generally and provide subject access to it. Additionally, employees should note that there is a qualified right of access by an employee to health data.

### 2.8.8  Manual Information

From time to time, requests may be received for access to manual data which are outside the requirements of the Act. In the interest of good employee relations, it is suggested that organisations should look upon such requests favourably and provide access where it is practical and realistic to do so.

### 2.8.9 Recommendations

— Procedures must be drawn up for handling subject access requests. These should specify the information required by the employer to identify the individual and locate the data required. The procedure should be understood by all the staff involved. Details of the procedures and any appropriate forms should be readily available to all employees.

— Personnel administrators must establish procedures to capture all data covered by the relevant registration including data held locally on personal computers.

— In the interest of good employee relations and employee co-operation in maintaining accurate data, it is recommended that no fee is charged to current employees making easily satisfied requests, such as from a main personnel records system, at reasonable intervals. Such data need not be a full historical record, but should contain all data that may be currently relevant. It should of course be made clear that this does not affect the employee's rights under the Act to have access to all data held under registration, including archive information.

### 2.9 THE EIGHTH PRINCIPLE

Appropriate security measures shall be taken against unauthorised access to, or alteration, disclosure or destruction of personal data and against accidental loss or destruction of personal data.

### 2.9.1 Interpretation

This principle applies to data users and computer bureaux and is concerned with data security, encompassing:

— unauthorised access either physically into the computer premises or into the software;

— the alteration, disclosure or destruction of data without the authority of the employer;

— the accidental loss or destruction of data either through negligence or through unreliable hardware, software, or back-up and recovery procedures.

The security needs should be determined in the light of the sensitivity of the data and the harm that could result from any of the breaches referred to by the principle. Attention should also be paid to the physical security of the computer installation, to security measures programmed into the software and to the reliability of staff accessing the data. Care should be taken that staff are selected on the basis of their competence. Sound induction and adequate training in the use of the system and associated procedures should be provided.

### 2.9.2  Physical Security

Buildings containing computer installations should be adequately protected against such contingencies as fire, flood and break-in. Access to installations, including micro-computers and desk-top or hand-held computers, should involve adequate security procedures, such as badges, passes or electronic key or card systems, to reduce the likelihood of unauthorised access. Screens should be positioned so that they cannot be read by visitors or unauthorised employees. When not in use or in out-of-work hours, procedures must be followed for locking up tapes, disks and printouts in a secure fireproof place.

### 2.9.3  Software Security

A range of factors need to be considered including:

— thorough testing of the reliability and integrity of the software to ensure that it performs to its specification;

— in-built checks to validate the input of the data;

— back-up and restore facilities to ensure the ability of the system to recover data;

— procedures requiring the duplication of data on a regular basis and their removal to a safe and secure place, eg to another site;

— thorough training of staff in the use of all relevant procedures relating to the system and their responsibilities for maintaining data privacy.

## 2.9.4  Access Controls

Factors to be considered include:

— controls on access to data by means of a system of passwords or other identifiers, changed at reasonably frequent intervals and when an employee leaves or changes responsibilities, which limit access to defined parts or levels of the system, as appropriate;

— clear policies and procedures regarding the issuing of passwords and clearly laid down responsibilities for monitoring the effectiveness of these procedures;

— audit facilities to check who is accessing the system and for what purpose.

Organisations also need to be aware of any security facilities incorporated in the system's software and of the terminal's characteristics, eg automatic blanking of screen when not in use.

## 2.9.5  Recommendations

— Personnel administrators should ensure that there are policies and procedures laid down regarding physical and software security. They should ensure that these are applied to all computer systems in their organisations that hold personal data, including, for example, personal computers operated independently by individual members of staff.

— Supervisory responsibility should be clearly defined to ensure that security procedures are followed and proper access to the system controlled.

— Personnel administrators should ensure that print-outs of personal data, including hard copy prints of screen displays, are disposed of in a way which maintains confidentiality.

— Where data are particularly sensitive, and are held by a computer bureau, this fact should be made known to the bureau and clearly specified in the contract between the parties.

# 3 Code of Practice for Computer Bureaux

## 3.1 INTRODUCTION

The Data Protection Act is an act to regulate the processing and use of information held on computer about individuals and services provided in respect of such information.

It gives rights to individuals about whom information is automatically processed. These rights are the right of access to personal information held on computers, the right to compensation for inaccuracy or loss of data, and the right to correction or erasure. The Act enabled the UK to ratify the Council of Europe Convention for the Protection of Individuals with Regard to the Automatic Processing of Personal Data.

The obligations of the Data Protection Act as regards computer bureaux are that each bureau should register (section 5(4) of the Act) that it should only disclose data as authorised by the data user (section 15) and that it should provide appropriate security measures in accordance with the Eighth Principle. Many computer bureaux also act as agents for their clients, in this case they will be limited to the processing and disclosure of data as set out in their clients' registered particulars.

Many computer bureaux will also handle data for their own purposes. With respect to such data, they will be data users. The Act requires data users, unless exempt, to register their data usage, to grant an individual access to his or her data and to comply with the set of eight data protection principles.

The code is intended to highlight the implications of the Act for a computer bureau and to give practical assistance on the adoption of good practice likely to ensure compliance with the Act and the maintenance of good practice to bodies providing commercial computer bureau services.

It has been developed jointly by the Computing Services Association and the National Computing Centre. It should be read in conjunction with guidelines and further information issued by the Data Protection Registrar and in the light of judgements by the Data Protection Tribunal and the higher courts. Organisations and individuals defined as data users are referred to other more appropriate codes of practice. (See Bibliography).

## 3.2  DEFINITIONS

The definitions are set out in section 1 of the Act and are further explained in the Registrar's Guideline 2, which should be consulted for clarification. Briefly the Act is concerned only with personal information recorded in a form in which it can be processed automatically.

The data user is defined as the organisation or individual responsible for controlling the content and use of a collection of personal data. This function will usually be carried out by the client of a computer bureau.

Section 1(6) defines a computer bureau thus:

> A person carries on a computer bureau if he provides other persons with services in respect of data, and a person provides such services if:
>
> a) as agent for other persons he causes data held by them to be processed . . . or
>
> b) he allows other persons the use of equipment in his possession for the processing . . . of data held by them.

The first part of the definition covers a person who is actively involved in automatically processing information controlled by others. The term 'agent' in this context means simply 'a person acting for others', rather than an agent in a contractual sense. Most companies providing a traditional computer bureau service to one or more clients will be acting as an agent for others, and will belong to this category.

The second part of the definition covers a person who, although taking no active part in the processing, allows others to use computer equipment in his possession. 'Possession' means exercising physical control of the equipment; it is not limited to ownership of a machine or disk. Processing, as covered by this point, will be carried out by the staff of the data user rather than of the computer bureau.

Many data users who have their own equipment will find that, for the purposes of the Data Protection Act, they are also acting as a computer bureau. This will be the case, for example, if they provide a computerised record-keeping service for others or have a reciprocal back-up arrangement with another user in case either computer fails.

## 3.3 SUMMARY OF THE RESPONSIBILITIES OF THE COMPUTER BUREAU

A person who runs a computer bureau must:

— register with the Office of the Data Protection Registrar;

— ensure that personal data is not disclosed without the authority of the person for whom services are provided;

— comply with the requirements of the Eighth Principle to take appropriate security measures in respect of the personal data held and processed.

The obligations of the computer bureau under the Act include not aiding the data user in any contravention of the Act.

## 3.4 SANCTIONS

Generally the requirements of the Act reflect the aims of the good computer bureau, which will wish to keep data secure and accurate, to limit disclosure and to maintain the confidence of the data user and the data subject. However, failure to observe the Eighth Principle may lead the Data Protection Registrar to issue an Enforcement Notice. The Enforcement Notice will specify the nature of the breach and, in general terms, what must be done to correct matters. Failure to comply with an Enforcement Notice will be an offence and may lead to fines and deregistration. A bureau that is deregistered will not be able to handle any personal data until a new application for registration has been accepted by the Registrar.

Failure to register or the unauthorised disclosure of personal data may also result in prosecution.

## 3.5   RELATIONSHIP OF DATA USERS AND THE COMPUTER BUREAU

The data user controls the use and content of the data, ie it is the body that updates the data as necessary and decides when processes are to be carried out. The data user is responsible for registration of data for each purpose and for ensuring that data are used only in accordance with the registered purpose.

The computer bureau will carry out processing on behalf of the data user or will allow the data user the use of equipment. The bureau should only be used to process data in accordance with the registered particulars. The bureau should also prevent any unauthorised disclosure and observe the Eighth Principle.

## 3.6   REGISTRATION

A computer bureau need only register under the Act if it carries out work with regard to personal data. Since most bureaux are not able to predict the contents of their work, it is sensible always to register.

Registration as a computer bureau only requires the applicant to complete details of name and address on a DPR1 or DPR4 application form for forwarding to the Office of the Data Protection Registrar (forms DPR1 and DPR4 are available from the Registrar's Office at the address given in the Appendix).

If the bureau is also a data user, a single application for registration as a data user and computer bureau may be made. An application for registration as a data user and computer bureau requires the applicant to provide purpose/subject/class/source/disclosure/transfer details for the personal data for which the bureau exercises control of content and use.

Once the application has been accepted, the bureau should ensure that the details of the register entry are kept up to date. Any changes to the registered particulars should be notified to the Registrar's Office on a DPR2 form (for Alteration or Removal of a Register Entry). An application to renew the register entry should be submitted every three years. The Registrar's Office will despatch a renewal reminder/application form prior to the expiry date.

An organisation which belongs to the first category of computer bureau above and is, therefore, acting as an agent of the person to whom it provides its services must not knowingly or recklessly depart from the terms of the data user's register entry, if any.

To minimise the possibility of a charge of recklessness, the bureau should require by contract an assurance from each customer that he is properly registered under the Act in respect of personal data held by him and processed by the bureau, and that he will not require the bureau to act outside the scope of his register entry. Any potential customer who will not give this contractual assurance should not be supplied with a bureau service.

An organisation which belongs to the second category of computer bureau defined above need not be concerned with the question of whether its customers have registered as data users or the contents of their register entries if they have registered.

## 3.7  DISCLOSURE

A computer bureau will normally handle data on behalf of the data user and return all input and output, in on-line or printed form, to the data user. The control of the data, input and output, will thus remain with the data user. However, a data user may sometimes wish the bureau to disclose output directly to save time. Examples of such disclosures may occur with pay details being sent directly to Inland Revenue, to DSS and to BACS or with replies to data subject access requests being sent to the data subject. A bureau that undertakes any such disclosure on behalf of the data user is acting as an agent of the data user. Since any unauthorised disclosure is an offence, care must be taken that any disclosure is permitted. A written authority from the data user should be requested before any disclosures to third parties are made. This authority will be in addition to the assurance that the functions required are covered by the data user's registered entries.

Unauthorised disclosure can be made accidentally due to lack of security or poor control. Adequate precautions must be taken against information in any form being disclosed by accident.

Personal data should not be used for demonstrations to prospective clients. Such demonstrations should make use of non-identifiable data.

Where a bureau uses a computer maintenance organisation to rectify hardware/software faults, it should advise the data user to whom it is providing a service to include disclosure code D206 on the appropriate register entry.

In the event of data media needing to be sent abroad for engineering repair, the bureau should advise the data user responsible for the data to include the appropriate country or territory in the overseas transfer section of the register entry.

## 3.8   DATA SUBJECT ACCESS

Data subjects have the right to approach a data user and request a copy of the data held about him or her. The individual is required to submit the request in writing to the data user. However, it is conceivable that a data subject may make his request through the computer bureau.

In view of the 40 day time limit for replying to a subject access request, the bureau should ensure that the request is passed on promptly to the appropriate individual within the data user organisation.

## 3.9   SECURITY

### 3.9.1   Introduction

Computer bureaux are required to comply with the Eighth Principle:

> Appropriate security measures shall be taken against unauthorised access to, or alteration, disclosure or destruction of personal data and accidental loss or destruction of personal data.

Computer bureaux should take appropriate care of any information while it is in their charge. This care should extend to software, back-up copies and information extracted from the data in the form of screens or print-out.

### 3.9.2   Interpretation

The principle covers the prevention of:

— unauthorised physical or logical access;

— the alteration, disclosure or destruction of data without the authority of the data user;

— the accidental loss or destruction of data because of unreliable hardware, software or back-up and recovery procedures.

In interpreting the principle, consideration should be given to security needs in the light of the sensitivity of the data and the harm that could result from any of the events referred to by the principle. Attention should be paid to the physical security of the computer installation, to security measures programmed into the software and to the reliability of staff using data. Procedures for staff selection, induction and training in the use of the system may need to be provided.

### 3.9.3  Physical Security

The building housing a computer installation should be adequately protected against such contingencies as fire, flood and break-in. Access to the installation should involve adequate security procedures, such as badges, passes or electronic card systems, to reduce the likelihood of unauthorised access.

If there are insufficient access controls on personal computers or terminals, the equipment should either be locked away when not in use or keyboard locks fitted.

Where VDU screens are situated in places visited by members of the public, or are visible from outside the building, they should be positioned so that they cannot be read by someone not authorised to do so.

When not in use, or during out-of-work hours, procedures must be followed for locking up tapes, disks and print-outs in a fireproof, secure place. Clients' data media must always, when not in use, be kept in a secure location.

### 3.9.4  Use of Media

Media belonging to a client and lodged at the premises of the computer bureau should not be used for the processing of data not appropriate to that client.

### 3.9.5  Software Security

A range of factors needs to be considered including the following:

— prevention of confusion of data provided by different clients sharing software;

— thorough training of staff in the use of all relevant procedures relating to the system and their responsibilities for maintaining data privacy.

### 3.9.6  Data Access Controls

Factors to be considered include the following:

— preventing unauthorised access to client's data by bureau staff;

— the use of passwords, or other identifiers, to limit access to defined parts or levels of the system;

— clear policies and procedures regarding the issuing, changing and deletion of identifiers and clearly laid down reponsibilities for monitoring the effectiveness of these procedures;

— audit facilities to check who is accessing the system and for what purpose;

— the provision of security features within the operating software.

### 3.9.7  Disposal of Media

Unwanted and out-of-date print-outs containing personal data must be returned to the client or disposed of securely by shredding or incineration. This applies to hard-copy screen prints, any specialised documents and computer listings; they must never be re-used for scrap paper.

Carbon paper and one-time printer ribbons must also be disposed of securely if they have been used in the production of personal data.

Where outside contractors are employed to remove stationery waste, there must be proper contractual arrangements for the secure disposal of that relating to personal data which the computer bureau should ensure are being observed.

### 3.9.8  Advising Clients of Security Arrangements

The computer bureau should provide sufficient security to a given standard and inform the data user of that standard. Data users should inform the bureau when any particularly sensitive data are to be handled. The bureau should only handle them if they can provide the appropriate level of security.

Bureau staff should be trained in all appropriate aspects of security and observance of the Data Protection Act.

# 4   Code of Practice for Customer and Supplier Administration

*Note by Data Protection Registrar*

*I welcome this valuable initiative taken by the National Computing Centre with support from the Department of Trade and Industry. I am pleased to note that the document has been developed in collaboration with the Chartered Institute of Management Accountants, the Institute of Internal Auditors, and the Institute of Purchasing and Supply and that these bodies will recommend to their members that they follow the guidance given.*

*Many different types of organisations across all sectors of the economy use personal data for customer and supplier administration. The guidance outlines practices which should assist them to comply with the data protection principles. The emphasis given to the practical application of the principles should prove particularly helpful.*

*Experience of data protection issues and of the practical application of the Act is developing rapidly. Data users should be aware, therefore, that the guidance given in this document is likely to need re-assessment from time to time.*

*I now look to data users to develop their own more detailed and specific procedures which will ensure that the data protection principles are met.*

## 4.1  INTRODUCTION

### 4.1.1  Purpose

This code is intended to assist those involved in the administration of customer and supplier records, eg sales orders, purchase orders and accounts, to comply with the Data Protection Act. The Act requires users of computerised personal data, unless exempt, to register their data usage, to grant an individual access to his or her data and to abide by the eight data protection principles. This code explains the principles of the Act in the context of customer and supplier administration. It is intended to help the data user to interpret the principles for his particular circumstances.

### 4.1.2  Scope

This code refers to customer and supplier administration data covered by the Data Protection Act, ie personal data recorded in a form in which they can be processed by equipment operating automatically, as defined in the Act, by or on behalf of a data user.

The definitions of the above terms are set out in section 1 of the Act, which should be consulted for clarification. Briefly, the Act is concerned only with computer-held data which relate to a living individual. The data subject is the individual to whom the data relate.

The data user is the organisation that controls the use and content of the data, whether it processes the data on its own equipment or makes use of another's processing facilities, ie a computer bureau. The term computer bureau refers to a person or organisation which provides data services to others, either by processing data for others by equipment operating automatically or by allowing others to use equipment in its possession to carry out such processing.

Processing is defined by the Act to mean amending, adding to, deleting or rearranging the data or extracting the information that forms the data.

### 4.1.3  Registered Purposes

This section sets out those of the Registrar's standard purposes which have been used to determine the area of activity addressed by this code.

In addition to the standard purposes described in detail below there are a number of further standard purposes involving a specialised form of customer and supplier administration. These include (but are not confined to) Standard Purposes P023 (Borrower Account/Credit Facilities Administration), P027 (Credit Card and Charge Card Administration), P024 (Investment/Deposit Account Administration). Data users may find reference to the guidance set out here of assistance in relation to these additional purposes to the extent that they involve operations similar to ones falling within the ambit of the code.

To simplify the registration process, the Registrar has devised a number of standard purposes. Those which are relevant in the context of this code are listed below.

### 4.1.3.1 Customer Administration

The use of data for sales administration purposes will normally be covered by standard purpose:

P013 Customer/Client Administration

> The administration of orders and accounts relating to customers or clients. This covers the provision of continuing services as well as discrete sales.

Purposes P014 and P015 are *alternative* versions of Customer/Client Administration and should be used where appropriate.

P014 Lending and Hire Services Administration

> The management of lending, leasing and hiring services involving the physical issue of items, materials or equipment, long term or short term. This purpose applies to libraries and other collections issuing books, tapes or other items; and to the companies or organisations involved in the hire of plant, tools, equipment, vehicles, software or other items.

P015 Reservations/Bookings and Ticket Issue

> The provision of reservation, booking or ticket issuing services. This purpose applies to industries such as travel, hotel and catering, leisure and entertainment.

### 4.1.3.2  Supplier Administration

The use of data for supplier administration purposes will normally be covered by standard purpose:

P008  Purchase/Supplier Administration

> The administration of supplies of goods or services to the data user, by whatever method of contract or payment, including subscriptions and standing orders as well as discrete purchases.

### 4.1.4  Other Sources of Guidance and Information

The Act itself is the definitive statement of the law. The guidance provided in this code should be read subject to the provisions of the Act and any decisions of the Data Protection Tribunal and the higher courts.

This code is only intended to provide guidance to organisations and bodies in the particular area of customer and supplier administration. Many data users may have other computerised activities. Readers are therefore advised to seek guidance on these other areas. Other sources of assistance include publications produced by the Registrar, the National Computing Centre and trade associations and representative bodies (see Bibliography).

Data users can also seek advice directly from the Registrar on how to comply with the Data Protection Act. Additionally they may find it helpful to refer queries on the Act to their trade association. A data user might also decide that it would be helful to seek advice from his internal and/or external auditors on how to develop procedures to meet the requirements of the Act.

### 4.1.5  Breaches of the Act

Generally, the requirements of the Act tie in closely with the aims of the good computer user who will wish to keep data secure and accurate, to limit disclosure to the right people and to keep the data subject informed.

Nevertheless, the Act does provide for sanctions against those who ignore its provisions. Failure to comply with an Enforcement Notice will be an offence and may lead to fines or deregistration.

Prosecution may also follow a failure to register or the use, collection transfer or disclosure of data beyond the registered particulars.

Similarly, data users should bear in mind that data subjects, who suffer damage as a result of inaccurate data, loss of data or unauthorised access to, destruction of or disclosure of data may take legal action to seek recompense.

### 4.1.6  Structure

In the remainder of this code the implication for sales and purchasing administration of each data protection principle is examined in turn.

An explanation of the meaning of each principle is provided together with advice and recommendations to ensure compliance.

There is an obligation on all data users to observe all the principles set out in Schedule 1 of the Act. There is an obligation on computer bureaux to observe the Eighth Principle which relates to data security.

## 4.2  THE FIRST PRINCIPLE

The information to be contained in personal data shall be obtained, and personal data shall be processed, fairly and lawfully.

### 4.2.1  Explanation

Anyone providing information should not be deceived or misled as to the purposes for which the data will be used or disclosed. Information is always treated as having been fairly obtained when the person from whom the information was obtained was authorised or requested by law to supply it.

Similarly, information disclosed by a person will always be treated as having been fairly obtained to the extent that the disclosure was required or authorised by law, even though the disclosure may not have been indicated to the data subject at the time the information was collected, eg information provided to the police when required or authorised by statute will be fairly disclosed.

Data held for historical, statistical or research purposes and not used in a way which causes or is likely to cause damage or distress will not be regarded as having been obtained unfairly merely because these uses were not specified to the person providing the information.

## 4.2.2 Fair Obtaining and Processing of Personal Data

Data collected for the purposes of supplier or customer administration should be obtained from reliable sources which must have been included in the registration details of the specific purpose.

Unless the individual supplying the information can reasonably be expected to appreciate the purposes for which the data user intends to use, or disclose, the information, the data user should provide an explanation before the information is obtained.

For example, the data which a retail customer provides, in order that goods which he has purchased can be delivered to his home, should not be used by the supplier to provide unrelated services without the customer's consent.

Further information on this subject may be found in Guideline 4 obtainable from the Office of the Data Protection Registrar.

## 4.2.3 Recommendations

— Data users should tell the data subject of the personal data which it is proposed to hold about him and any uses to which the data may be put.

— Data users should adopt a clear policy on the confidentiality of data.

— Data users should collect personal information only for legitimate business purposes.

## 4.3 THE SECOND PRINCIPLE

Personal data shall be held only for one or more specified and lawful purposes.

### 4.3.1 Explanation

This principle is complied with by registration provided that the data user only processes data in accordance with the purposes registered.

### 4.3.2 Customer and Supplier Administration Data

Uses of data which might be expected to form part of customer and supplier administration are given below and are derived from the

Registrar's standard purpose descriptions referred to above at Section 4.1.3.

Typical uses of customer data which might be expected are:

### 4.3.2.1 *P013 (Customer/Client Administration)*

— recording and processing of orders and payments (sales ledger);

— credit checking or rating;

— control and monitoring of after sales service or maintenance;

— dealing with customer complaints or enquiries;

— analysis for management purposes and statutory returns.

### 4.3.2.2 *P014 (Lending and Hire Services Administration)*

— the maintenance of reservation/booking and recall systems, together with any associated ticket and account administration;

— processing of payments;

— credit checking or rating;

— dealing with customer complaints and enquiries;

— analysis for management purposes and statutory returns.

### 4.3.2.3 *P015 (Reservations, Bookings and Ticket Issue)*

— the recording of customer/client requirements and preferences;

— the control of agencies for this type of service;

— processing of payments;

— credit checking or rating;

— dealing with customer complaints or enquiries;

— analysis for management purposes and statutory returns.

### 4.3.2.4 *Supplier Data*

Standard Purpose P008, Purchase/Supplier Administration, includes the following typical activities:

— the identification, checking and selection of suppliers;

— ordering of goods and services;

— recording and processing of goods received;

— recording and processing of payments made (purchase ledger);

— monitoring supplier performance;

— analysis for management purposes and statutory returns.

### 4.3.3  Exemption from the Act

Personal data are exempt from the whole of the Act if they are held by a data user *only* for one, or more, of the following accounts purposes:

— keeping accounts relating to any business or other activity carried on by the data user;

— keeping records of purchases, sales or other transactions for the purpose of ensuring that the requisite payments are made by or to the data user in respect of those transactions;

— keeping records of purchases, sales or other transactions for the purpose of making financial or management forecasts to assist the data user in the conduct of any business or activity carried on by him.

If the data are used for any other purpose, for example, rating supplier performance or keeping credit ratings on customers, the exemption would be lost.

If the data user is satisfied that his processing is limited to the specified purposes, he must also bear in mind that to qualify for exemption, personal data may only be disclosed:

— for audit purposes;

— for the purpose of giving information about the data user's financial affairs;

— in circumstances covered by one of the exemptions from the non-disclosure provisions of the Act given in Section 4.4.3 below.

An illustration of where the 'accounts' exemption would be lost is when a data user makes a disclosure of personal data to an outside computer maintenance firm during the course of maintenance work on the data user's computer facilities, without the prior consent to the disclosure by the individuals to which the data refers.

### 4.3.4  Recommendations

— Sales administration should normally be registered under Standard Purpose P013 unless the specialised Purposes P014 or P015 apply. The additional purposes should be registered when applicable.

— Supplier administration should be registered under Standard Purpose P008.

— Managers of both functions must ensure that no processing takes place which is not covered by the registered particulars. Managers should also ensure that registered particulars are kept up to date and are amended or renewed as new computerised activities become operational.

— The accounts and mailing list exemptions are only likely to be used by very small organisations and then only in exceptional circumstances. The restrictions are such as to make it very difficult not to breach the exemption rules, for example if comments such as 'last delivery below standard' or 'cash with order only' are recorded, exemption will be lost.

## 4.4   THE THIRD PRINCIPLE

Personal data held for any purpose or purposes shall not be used or disclosed in any manner incompatible with that purpose or those purposes.

### 4.4.1   Explanation

This principle will be complied with provided that data are only used for the purpose(s) specified and disclosed only to those described in the data user's register entry.

### 4.4.2   Disclosures of Personal Data

Reference by the Act to 'disclosing' data includes disclosing information extracted from the data. A disclosure occurs whenever the data, or information extracted from the data, are passed to someone other than the data user; whether this is done orally, in writing or by showing the other person a print-out or a screen on which the information is displayed.

With some exceptions (4.4.3 below), disclosures of personal data can only be made to the persons described in the disclosure section of the data user's entry. Other disclosures may result in an action for personal damages by a data subject against a data user.

If the data are to be transmitted overseas, the countries or territories involved must be named in the registered entry.

### 4.4.3 Exemptions

In certain circumstances, personal data may be disclosed even though the disclosure has not been registered. Data may always be disclosed:

— to the data subject, to the data subject's authorised agent or at the request of the data subject;

— to the employees or agents of the data user to enable them to perform their duties as employees or agents;

— for the purpose of obtaining legal advice, or in the course of legal proceedings in which the person making the disclosure is a party or a witness;

— for the purposes of the assessment or collection of any tax or duty; the prevention or detection of crime; the apprehension or prosecution of offenders: but only where not to make the disclosure would be likely to prejudice one of those purposes;

— for national security reasons;

— when required urgently for the prevention of injury or damage to the health of any person;

— when required by statute, by any rule of law or by any order of the court.

When making disclosures under any of these exemptions, a manager must be satisfied that it is one which complies with the requirements of the particular non-disclosure exemption. For example, where a disclosure is made to the police for a crime prevention purpose, it would be advisable to ensure that it is only done on the basis of a written statement provided by a senior police officer indicating that it is his belief that the disclosure falls within the terms of the exemption.

### 4.4.4  Recommendations

— Sales and purchasing managers should lay down procedures and educate their staff and agents to ensure that the use and disclosure of personal data conform to the registered particulars.

— Managers should complete the Registrar's standard disclosure box D206, covering disclosures to suppliers and providers of goods or services. Inclusion of this disclosure covers those occasions when data may be inadvertently disclosed when a computer engineer is rectifying a machine malfunction.

— Firms with overseas offices to which they transfer data will need to include such transfer on their application for registration.

— Data users should adopt a clear policy on the confidentiality of all data relating to their customers and suppliers.

## 4.5  THE FOURTH PRINCIPLE

Personal data held for any purpose or purposes shall be adequate, relevant and not excessive in relation to that purpose or those purposes.

### 4.5.1  Explanation

This principle is aimed at ensuring that the personal data held for a particular purpose are sufficient, but not more than sufficient, for that purpose.

### 4.5.2  Adequacy and Relevance

In order to comply with this principle, sales and purchasing functions should review objectively what information is gathered about individuals and whether it is sufficient, relevant and not excessive for the purpose.

Careful consideration should be given to avoid the collection of information which cannot be fully justified. Information which is gathered just in case it might be useful might well breach this principle as being irrelevant or excessive for the purpose.

Customer data are concerned with orders received, goods and services provided, delivery and invoice addresses, accounts due, amounts paid, credit ratings and financial references, complaints and service calls.

Supplier data are concerned with orders placed, goods and services received, supplier addresses, accounts due, amounts paid, quality control and supplier performance.

No definitive list can be provided, since the detail depends on business circumstances. For data to be adequate and relevant it must provide complete, but not excessive, information for carrying out the registered purposes.

For example, Personal Habits (Registrar's data class C013) are unlikely to be considered relevant to Purpose P013 (Customer/Client Administration) in the normal business context, but may be relevant to P015 (Reservations, Bookings and Ticket Issues), ie smoking/non-smoking, vegetarian, etc. Similarly, in the context of supplier administration, C012 (Physical Description) is unlikely to be considered relevant.

Computerised data may be supplemented by manual information, so this will be pertinent to any assessment of adequacy of data.

### 4.5.3  Recommendation

— Sales and purchasing managers should consider the data which are held in the light of the full range of services received or provided and should be aware that they might be required to provide an objective explanation of why one or more items of data are being held.

### 4.6  THE FIFTH PRINCIPLE

Personal data shall be accurate and, where necessary, kept up to date.

### 4.6.1  Explanation

Data are only considered inaccurate for the purpose of this principle if they are incorrect or misleading as to any matter of fact.

Updating is required only 'where necessary' so that data which do not change, such as the record of a transaction, or when an account was opened are unlikely to be in need of updating but must be accurate at the time of entry. Other items which are used to make current judgements need to be up to date. For example a credit rating may need to be confirmed before a new contract is agreed. Recording the date of entry or update will assist in ensuring that data are accurate and kept up to date.

### 4.6.2  Steps to Ensure Accuracy and Currency

Bearing in mind the sensitivity of the data and the harm that might result if incorrect, a number of steps can be taken to ensure accuracy and to provide a defence against claims regarding inaccurate data. They include:

— reasonable checks on the accuracy of data provided by reference to original documentation, ie proper input checking procedures;

— checks built into the software to help ensure that data are validated on entry and comply with certain predetermined criteria; eg check digit validation of account numbers, match payments made to invoices;

— the provision of order acknowledgements and statements on a regular basis, with the opportunity to raise queries, investigate them and correct the record where appropriate;

— the prompt investigation and correction of errors in data and faults in software.

### 4.6.3  Recommendations

— Sales and purchasing managers should seek to verify information obtained by reference to documentary evidence.

— Operating procedures and software design should incorporate controls to ensure that only valid data are accepted and recorded and that they are on the correct record.

— Queries and complaints about inaccuracies should be handled quickly and sympathetically.

## 4.7  THE SIXTH PRINCIPLE

Personal data held for any purpose or purposes shall not be kept for longer than is necessary for that purpose or those purposes.

### 4.7.1  Explanation

Data which are held for historical, statistical or research purposes may be kept indefinitely, provided that the data are used in such a way that no damage or distress is, or is likely to be, caused to any data subject.

Data retained for other purposes should be subject to regular review and, when appropriate, deleted.

### 4.7.2 Present and Past Customers and Suppliers

Reasons for keeping data about present or past customers and suppliers include acting on subsequent legal claims, the requirements of legislation (eg VAT) and audit.

Where statutory limitation periods apply these provide guidance on the appropriate periods for holding certain data, eg financial data must be retained for at least six years for tax purposes and, in some instances, longer. Where they do not apply, judgements will need to be made about how long data should be held; holding data just in case it might be useful in the future is not permitted. There must be a specified period for reviewing data.

Good practice suggests that data on the goods and services received or provided should be held for at least the current and previous trading years, or for one year after the expiration of a contract, but this must depend very much on the nature of the business and the frequency at which orders might be expected to be received or goods or services delivered.

What constitutes a 'past customer or supplier' must again depend upon the nature of the business and the frequency of trading. In most instances dormant personal accounts will be deleted at the end of each financial year, whilst in others it could be quite justifiable to hold summarised details of a customer and the last order placed, even though that may have been five years ago.

In all cases, the length of time various classes of data should be held should be discussed with both the internal and external auditors.

### 4.7.3 Prospective Customers and Suppliers

Where data are collected concerning prospective customers or suppliers in advance of an order being placed and that order subsequently does not materialise, the data should not be retained longer than might be considered reasonable for the purpose for which they were originally collected. Alternatively the data should be reviewed regularly to ensure currency.

For example, a builder who collects personal data as the basis of a quotation for constructing a house, who retains data about the customer despite the fact that the contract is placed with a competitor, would be in breach of the Sixth Principle. If the client's architect had also collected personal data about potential builders, he, too, should erase the data once the contract is placed.

### 4.7.4  Recommendations

— Sales and purchasing managers should develop and keep under regular review a policy, in conjunction with their organisation's internal and external auditors, on how long records will be held and in what detail in order to meet statutory claims or legitimate business needs.

— Deletions should be carried out at appropriate intervals to remove data that are no longer required.

— Even though the Act provides that data held for historical, statistical or research purposes may be kept indefinitely, it is good practice to depersonalise such data as early as possible.

## 4.8  THE SEVENTH PRINCIPLE

An individual shall be entitled:

a) at reasonable intervals and without undue delay or expense:

    i) to be informed by any data user whether he holds personal data of which that individual is the subject, and

    ii) to access to any such data held by a data user; and

b) where appropriate, to have such data corrected or erased.

### 4.8.1  Explanation

The principle should be interpreted by reference to section 21 of the Act. Section 21 is explained in some detail in the Registrar's Guideline 5. 'Reasonable' intervals between access requests will be interpreted in the light of the nature of the data, their purpose and the frequency with which they are updated. The correction or erasure of data is appropriate only where necessary to comply with other data protection principles.

### 4.8.2  Data to be Provided

All data, current and historical, held on an individual customer or supplier, including both facts and opinions, such as credit-worthiness, fall within the definitions of personal data.

It should be noted that data coming under the overall description of customer or supplier information may be held on more than one system within the organisation and may also include data held by line managers, eg at stores or service depots, on desk-top computers.

Where information about an individual is kept and it is not, nor intended to be, processed by reference to that individual, then it will not be personal data falling within the scope of the Act. However, the use of 'key-word' search software or some other means to pin-point data relating to an individual would make such data personal data within the Act.

Access need not be provided to what the Act terms the 'intentions' of the data user. Intentions may, for instance, relate to specific contracts to be placed or terminated, planned price changes or discount terms.

Where data, to which access is being provided, contains a reference identifying an individual other than the data subject, the data identifying that individual need not be disclosed unless the other individual has consented to the disclosure. However, the data user should still give as much information as possible to the data subject without revealing the identity of the other individual. This may involve editing the material to remove names or other identifying features.

Data held only for statistical purposes or research are exempt from the subject access provisions on the condition that the resulting statistics or the results of the research do not identify individuals, and that the data are not used or disclosed for any other purpose. If it is impractical to depersonalise the data then sales and purchasing managers should establish policies to ensure that the identities are not revealed.

For ease of administration and the furthering of good relations, it may well be considered best to give the data subject access rights to all the personal data held except in very exceptional circumstances.

### 4.8.3  Requests in Writing

Data users are only required to respond to written requests and are entitled to request reasonable further information to help locate the required records such as relevant reference numbers, office/department dealt with, representatives' names, nature of goods or services required/provided.

If the data user has more than one register entry, the data subject should state to which of those entries his request relates. In the interest of good relations, the data subject should be offered guidance on the relevance of each register entry to enable him to select the appropriate ones for each access.

A data user is entitled to charge a fee, subject to a statutory maximum, for providing subject access. At present (November 1989) the maximum fee is set at £10. A separate fee is legally chargeable for access to each registered entry.

### 4.8.4  Response

Once a request has been received the data user is obliged to reply within 40 days. The period does not commence until the data user has received all the information reasonably required to identify the individual requiring access and to locate the data.

During the time between receiving the request and replying to it, any normal amendments, insertions or deletions may be made to the data. However, no special changes should be made simply because the request has been received.

The data should be provided to the individual in written form and should be intelligible, with any coded information fully explained.

### 4.8.5  Identification of the Enquirer

In order to prevent inadvertent disclosure to an unauthorised person, the identity of the enquirer should be established. One means of establishing the bona fides of an enquirer is to ask for information which can be checked against details in the data subject's record.

### 4.8.6  Identification of the Data Required

To establish the data required, the enquirer should be asked to quote an appropriate reference. This could be an account number or, for customers, an invoice number. For suppliers the number of an order or of a remittance advice would be suitable.

Enquirers should be asked for any additional information which may help to identify the data in which they are interested. This will help to locate the less obvious records that may be held on micros and personal computers.

A data user is entitled to ask for information which he reasonably requires to locate the data requested. He may ask for additional information which would be helpful, though not reasonably required, but he should make it clear to the data subject that he does not have to supply these extra details.

### 4.8.7 Manual Information

Manually held information which has not been processed by computer lies outside the scope of the Act and this code. However, from time to time, requests may be received for access to manual data. It is suggested that organisations should look upon such requests favourably and provide access where it is practical and realistic to do so.

### 4.8.8 Recommendations

— Procedures must be drawn up for handling subject access requests. These should specify the information required to help identify the individual and locate the data required, including archived data and that held on PCs in departments, stores and other remote sites. The procedures should be understood by all staff involved. It may be helpful to draw up a standard request form. Details of the procedures should be made available to customers and suppliers who may wish to access the data held about them.

— Where practical, documents such as customer statements should contain as much information as is feasible, provided the document is always sent to the customer or his authorised agent. The provision of such data will not affect the data subject's right to all personal data held.

— When responding to a subject access request, the sensitivity of the data is a factor to be considered in determining how much evidence of identity should be sought.

## 4.9 THE EIGHTH PRINCIPLE

Appropriate security measures shall be taken against unauthorised access to, or alteration, disclosure or destruction of personal data and against accidental loss or destruction of personal data.

### 4.9.1 Explanation

This principle applies to both data users and computer bureaux and is concerned with the issue of data security, encompassing the prevention of:

— unauthorised access to personal data either by physical entry to premises or by logical access;

— the disclosure or destruction of data without the authority of the data user;

— the accidental loss or destruction of data because of human error, unreliable hardware, software or back-up and recovery procedures.

In interpreting the principle, consideration should be given to security needs in the light of the sensitivity of the data and the harm that could result from any of the events referred to by the principle. Attention should be paid to the physical security of the computer installation, to security measures programmed into the software and to the reliability of staff using data. Procedures for staff selection, induction and training in the use of the system may need to be provided.

### 4.9.2 Physical Security

The building housing a computer installation should be adequately protected against such contingencies as fire, flood and break-in. Access to the installation should involve adequate security procedures, such as badges, passes or electronic card systems, to reduce the likelihood of unauthorised access.

If there are insufficient access controls on personal computers or terminals, the equipment should either be locked away when not in use or keyboard locks fitted.

Where VDU screens are situated in places visited by members of the public, or are visible from outside the building, they should be positioned so that they cannot be read by someone not unauthorised to do so.

When not in use, or during out-of-work hours, procedures must be followed for locking up tapes, disks and print-outs in a fireproof, secure place.

### 4.9.3 Software Security

A range of factors needs to be considered including the following:

— thorough testing of the reliability and integrity of the software to ensure that it performs to its specification;

— in-built checks to validate the input of data;

— back-up and restore facilities to ensure the ability of the system to recover data;

— procedures requiring the duplication of data on a regular basis and their removal to a safe and secure place, eg to another site;

— thorough training of staff in the use of all relevant procedures relating to the system and their responsibilities for maintaining data privacy.

### 4.9.4 Data Access Controls

Factors to be considered include the following:

— the use of passwords, or other identifiers, to limit access to defined parts or levels of the system on a 'need to know' basis;

— clear policies and procedures regarding the issuing, changing and deletion of passwords and clearly laid down responsibilities for monitoring the effectiveness of these procedures;

— audit facilities to check who is accessing the system and for what purpose;

— the provision of security features within the operating software.

### 4.9.5 Disposal of Media

Unwanted out-of-date print-outs containing personal data must be disposed of securely by shredding or incineration. This applies to hard-copy screen prints, any specialised documents and computer listings; they must never be re-used for scrap paper. Carbon paper and one-time printer ribbons must also be disposed of securely if they have been used in the production of personal data.

Where outside contractors are employed to remove stationery waste, there must be proper contractual arrangements for the secure disposal of that relating to personal data and the data user must satisfy himself that they are being complied with.

Where magnetic media are disposed of, any personal data must be completely overwritten; the deletion of the file or record index is not sufficient.

### 4.9.6  Compensation for Loss or Unauthorised Disclosure

A claim for compensation can be made by a data subject to a court against a data user or a computer bureau, which is involved in the processing of personal data which relates to him, if as a result of loss, or unauthorised access to, or unauthorised destruction or disclosure of his data, he has suffered damage. However, no compensation is payable if the data user or computer bureau can prove that all such care was taken as was reasonably required to prevent the loss, access, destruction or disclosure.

### 4.9.7  Recommendations

— Where data are particularly sensitive and are held by a computer bureau, this fact should be made known to the bureau and clearly specified in the contract between the parties.

— The physical security of the computing environment should be such as to reduce the opportunities of unauthorised access to the equipment and there should be adequate precautions against theft of either the computing equipment or its associated storage or output media, as well as fire, flood or other disasters.

— The logical security should be such as to reduce the opportunities for unauthorised access to, amendment or destruction of, the personal data held.

— All copies of personal data either for input to the computer system or output, or obtained from the system, whether recorded on paper, microfilm or computer readable media, should be held secure from unauthorised access and securely destroyed or erased when they are no longer required.

— All personal data should be secured by adequate back-up copies to allow recovery from system failure. Where the personal data are of a particularly sensitive, extensive, potentially damaging or distressing nature, off-site storage of back-up copies should be considered to cope with extensive damage to the facilities at the location of the system.

— Information about an employee's responsibility for complying with the Act should be included in the contract of employment of any staff whose job provides access to personal data. Details of any disciplinary sanctions which will be applied, should he fail to comply, should also be provided.

— Where a computer bureau is used for processing, it should be provided with a list of disclosures which the data user authorises it to make.

# 5 Code of Practice for Pharmacists

## 5.1 INTRODUCTION

### 5.1.1 Purpose

This code is intended to assist pharmacists, both community and hospital, to comply with the Data Protection Act. The Act requires users of computerised personal data, unless exempt, to register their use of data, to grant access to the data to the individual concerned and to abide by the eight data protection principles. This code explains the principles of the Act in the context of pharmacy. It is intended to help the pharmacist, in his role as a data user, to interpret the principles for his particular circumstances.

### 5.1.2 Scope

The Data Protection Act is concerned only with personal data about identifiable living individuals processed by, or on behalf of, a data user. The definitions of these terms are set out in section 1 of the Act and are explained in the Registrar's Guideline 2, which may be consulted for clarification. Personal data includes any statement of fact or opinion about the individual but not any indication of the intentions of the data user in respect of that individual.

A pharmacist who controls the content and use of a collection of personal data is defined as a data user irrespective of whether the data is processed at the pharmacy or is processed externally by a computer bureau.

The term computer bureau applies to a person or organisation which provides data services to others, either by processing data for others or by allowing others to use equipment in its possession to carry out such processing.

A data subject means an individual who is the subject of personal data, eg patient, pharmaceutical representative.

Processing is defined by the Act to mean amending, adding to, deleting or re-arranging the data or extracting from the information that contains the data.

### 5.1.3  Registration

Any pharmacist who uses a computer to maintain patient medication records needs to register (see 5.3.3 below).

Many pharmacists work in partnership with other pharmacists or, in Scotland only, others. Where a name has been adopted for the purposes of accounting for shared services, eg Smith & Jones (Dispensing Chemists), this will be registered on form DPR1 at A2 as the name of the firm. The names of the individual partners are registered at A5. Whenever a new partner joins, or an existing partner leaves, the Registrar must be notified.

In addition to providing the names of the data users, one person must be nominated as data co-ordinator to be responsible for data protection. This is the person to whom subject access requests will be addressed and should preferably be one of the partners.

### 5.1.4  Registered Purposes

To simplify the registration process, the Data Protection Registrar has defined a number of 'Standard Purposes'. For each standard purpose, a general description is given, together with examples of typical activities which would fall within the scope of that purpose.

The use of data by pharmacists will normally be covered by standard purpose:

P062: The provision of patient care in NHS hospitals or community services, family practice or in private health care institutions,

which includes the following typical activities:

— the administration of patient records;

— the provision of general medical services;

— other medical, dental, pharmaceutical, nursing or ophthalmic treatment or care;

— pathology or other investigative services;

— diagnosis, therapy, rehabilitation, preventative care, screening and follow-up health services;

— analysis for management purposes and statutory returns.

In community pharmacies the records will normally consist of details of medicines supplied.

When registering under Purpose P062 the data user must indicate if data for any of the following specific purposes is held:

— genetic services;

— contraceptive services;

— abortion services;

— infertility services;

— care/treatment of persons suffering from:

- mental illness;

- addiction;

- sexually transmitted diseases.

Where health care administration is carried out using computers, the registration should include:

P067: The administration of health care services in the NHS and private sector,

which typically covers:

— organisation of in-patient, out-patient and family practitioner services;

— identification of patients;

— scheduling appointments and admissions;

— administration in connection with nursing, pharmacy, pathology and other investigative services;

— provision of health education information;

— financial administration including billing of patients and payment of fees;

— analysis for management purposes and statutory returns.

The increased opportunity for personal research, which computerised records provides, means that pharmacists should consider the need to register standard purpose:

P016: Research or statistical analysis in all fields, including scientific, technical, health, social, economic or market research.

Typical activities are:

— the identification of subjects for survey or analysis;

— collection or abstraction of data including the distribution of questionnaires and telephone or face-to-face interviews;

— analysis, modelling or simulation;

— evaluation of behaviour, attitudes or characteristics;

— the output/presentation of results or findings;

— analysis for management purposes and statutory returns.

If this purpose is registered, the general nature of the research, eg health, must be described. Health includes epidemiological research, clinical trials, biomedical research, research into prevention, prognosis and treatment of disease.

When deciding whether to register under Purpose P016 the pharmacist should consider whether the data are necessary for other purposes and are used for research only in support of those other purposes. In that case a separate registration under Purpose P016 is not necessary. If, on the other hand, data are collected specifically for research, registration under Purpose P016 is required.

A pharmacist may control data in support of his own objectives or, if a National Health Service contractor, may only provide information to the Prescription Pricing Authority (PPA). If his sole use of data is the provision of the data to the PPA, the pharmacist is not a data user.

The Data Protection Registrar has published 'Notes to Help You Apply for Registration' which should be consulted when registering.

### 5.1.5  Other Sources of Guidance and Information

The Act itself is the definitive statement of the law. The guidance provided in this code should be read subject to the provisions of the Act.

A series of eight Guidelines has been published by the Data Protection Registrar to inform individuals of their rights under the Act and to help those who process personal data to understand their obligations.

This code of practice is solely concerned with the use of computers by pharmacists. Pharmacists who use a computer for administrative purposes not concerned with patient care may also need to consult one, or more, of the guides which have been published (see Bibliography).

Those working within the National Health Service hospital service should consult the NHS Data Protection Handbook. Each health authority (or health board in Scotland) will have its own policy and pharmacists are advised to consult their pharmaceutical officer.

Further guidance on the interpretation of the Act is also available directly from the Data Protection Registrar and from the Data Protection Co-ordinator of the Royal Pharmaceutical Society (see Appendix).

### 5.1.6  Supervision and Enforcement of the Act

Generally, the requirements of the Act tie in closely with the aims of the good computer user who will wish to keep data secure and accurate, to limit disclosure to the right people and to keep the patient informed.

Nevertheless the Act does provide for sanctions against those who ignore its provisions. Where the Registrar believes that a principle has not been observed he may issue a Notice to the pharmacist concerned. Failure to comply with a Registrar's Notice will be an offence and may lead to deregistration and prosecution.

Prosecution may also follow a failure to register or the use, collection, transfer or disclosure of data beyond the registered particulars.

Any successful prosecution may result in a fine being imposed.

Pharmacists should bear in mind that patients who suffer damage as a result of inaccurate data or unauthorised alteration or disclosure of their data may take legal action to seek recompense.

## 5.1.7 Structure

In the remainder of this code each data protection principle is considered in turn. In each case its applicability to pharmaceutical systems is considered further.

There is an obligation on all data users to observe all the principles set out in Schedule 1 of the Act. There is an obligation on computer bureaux and data users alike to observe the Eighth Principle which relates to data security.

The observation of professional standards may, on occasion, indicate a need to go beyond the actual requirements of the Act. A number of recommendations contained in this code are probably in excess of the strict legal requirements of the Act.

## 5.2 THE FIRST PRINCIPLE

The information to be contained in personal data shall be obtained, and personal data shall be processed, fairly and lawfully.

## 5.2.1 Explanation

A patient providing information should not be deceived or misled as to the purposes for which the data will be used or disclosed. Information is always treated as having been fairly obtained when the person from whom the information was obtained was authorised or required by law to supply it.

Similarly, information disclosed by a person will always be treated as having been fairly obtained to the extent that the disclosure was required and authorised by law, even though the disclosure may not have been indicated to the data subject at the time the information was collected, eg information provided to the police when required or authorised by statute will be fairly disclosed.

Fairness in respect of obtaining and processing information will need to be judged by reference to the purposes of the data user and the consequences for the data subject.

Data held for historical, statistical or research purposes and not used in a way which causes or is likely to cause damage or distress will not be regarded as having been obtained unfairly merely because these uses were not specified to the person providing the information.

### 5.2.2  Fair Collection and Use of Data

Data collected for the purposes of provision of patient care should be obtained from reliable sources which must have been included in the registration details of the specific purpose. In the case of patient medication record systems the source is normally the patient and/or the doctor.

### 5.2.3  Recommendations

— Since the computer is probably sited in the dispensary away from view the patient may not be aware that the pharmacist maintains medication records. Pharmacists should tell the patient of the personal data which it is proposed to hold about him and any sources from which they may be obtained and any disclosures which may be made. In a busy pharmacy there may not always be time to do this. In such circumstances, it is desirable to display an explanatory notice.

— Pharmacists should only collect data when the patient understands the purposes for which the data are collected.

— Pharmacists should establish suitable policies for data collection for their staff and colleagues and ensure that they understand their obligations.

— Free text fields are a characteristic of some patient medical record systems and hold particular dangers as they allow the opportunity for derogatory and potentially damaging remarks to be entered without being subject to any checks for accuracy. Pharmacists should establish procedures to ensure that only authenticated originators can make such entries and that the entry records their identity and the date on which the entry was made.

### 5.3  THE SECOND PRINCIPLE

Personal data shall be held only for one or more specified and lawful purposes.

### 5.3.1  Explanation

This principle is readily complied with if the pharmacist:

— registers with the Office of the Data Protection Registrar;

— registers all the purposes for which personal data is to be held or used;

— establishes procedures to ensure that the Registrar is immediately notified of any new purposes for holding personal data.

### 5.3.2 Exemption from the Requirement to Register

Where the data are used *solely* for the production of dispensing labels and are not retained for processing by reference to the individual, registration is not required.

Registration is not required for data consisting only of name and address and used solely for distribution and recording distribution. However, this exemption only applies if every data subject is asked whether he objects and does not do so.

The Registrar's Guideline 6 describes the exemptions. In practice, the constraints on what data may be held and what disclosures made in connection with these applications are such that registration is strongly recommended.

### 5.3.3 Recommendations

— Pharmacists should register under Standard Purpose P062 and, if necessary, P067 and P016.

— Pharmacists must ensure that no processing takes place which is not covered by the register entry. As new systems become operational, the registered particulars should be reviewed and, if appropriate, amended.

— Each registration under purposes P062 and P067 may carry in the continuation section: 'disclosure will be made in accordance with the Royal Pharmaceutical Society of Great Britain Code of Ethics'.

### 5.4 THE THIRD PRINCIPLE

Personal data held for any purpose or purposes shall not be used or disclosed in any manner incompatible with that purpose or those purposes.

### 5.4.1  Explanation

This principle will be complied with provided that data are only used for the purpose(s) specified and disclosed only to those described in the data user's register entry. The Data Protection Act is not a confidentiality act but it does require data users to be open about any disclosures that they may wish to make.

### 5.4.2  Disclosures of Personal Data

Reference by the Act to 'disclosing' data includes disclosing information extracted from the data if the patient's identity is indicated or could be inferred. A disclosure occurs whenever the data, or information extracted from the data, are passed to someone other than the pharmacist, his staff or agents, whether this is done orally, or in writing or by showing the other person a print-out or a screen on which the information is displayed.

It is usually established policy that all staff, who have access to personal information during the course of their work, should not pass it on to others unless it is necessary for the discharge of their responsibilities. The Data Protection Act reinforces such policies as, with some exceptions (5.4.3 below), disclosures of personal data can only be made to the persons described in the data user's entry which relates to that data. Any other disclosures could result in prosecution.

Those working within the National Health Service hospital service should refer requests for disclosure of information to the Health Authority/Board Data Protection Co-ordinator.

The Act only provides protection for data about living persons. However, before disclosing data about a dead patient, a pharmacist must consider whether the disclosure would identify any third parties who are still alive.

### 5.4.3  Exemptions

In certain circumstances, patient data may be disclosed even though the disclosure has not been registered. Patient data may always be disclosed:

— to the patient, to the patient's authorised agent or at the request of the patient;

- to the employees or agents of the pharmacist to enable them to perform their duties as employees or agents;
- for the purpose of obtaining legal advice, or in the course of legal proceedings in which the pharmacist is a party or a witness;
- for the purpose of the assessment or collection of any tax or duty (which may include prescription fees) but only if such use would be prejudiced by a failure to disclose.
- when required urgently for the prevention of injury or damage to the health of any person;
- when required by statute, by any rule of law or by any order of the court.

When making disclosures under any of these exemptions, the provider must be completely satisfied about the legitimacy of the third parties involved and seek documentary evidence, where appropriate.

### 5.4.4  Recommendations

- Pharmacists should lay down procedures and train their staff to ensure that the use and disclosure of personal data conforms to the registered particulars.
- Staff should sign a contract which includes a passage along the following lines:

  Your attention is drawn to the confidential nature of this post. Disclosures of confidential information or disclosures of any personal data can result in prosecution for an offence under the Data Protection Act or an action for civil damages under the same Act. This is in addition to any disciplinary action taken by your employer which might include dismissal.

- Disclosure to suppliers, providers of goods or services (D206) should always be registered and the contract with the computer hardware and software maintenance companies should include a confidentiality clause.
- In order to avoid unauthorised disclosure, particularly when the pharmacist is absent, computer terminals should be securely protected by appropriate location in the dispensary and password

or physical controls on the terminals. Passwords should be changed regularly.

— Procedures should be established to record any occasions on which disclosures are made under the provisions of the exemption circumstances.

## 5.5 THE FOURTH PRINCIPLE

Personal data held for any purpose or purposes shall be adequate, relevant and not excessive in relation to that purpose or those purposes.

### 5.5.1 Explanation

This principle is aimed at ensuring that the personal data held for a particular purpose are sufficient, but not more than sufficient, for that purpose.

### 5.5.2 Adequacy and Relevance

The problem of ensuring the adequacy and relevance of information for a particular purpose is that health care is frequently akin to a detection process. The most unlikely pieces of information can turn out to provide the critical clues to drug interaction or prescription errors when they appear in combination with other apparently unconnected items. It is no function of the Data Protection Act to inhibit the caring professions in their search to provide better patient care. However, the more sensitive the information and the greater the volume of information collected, the more security problems are faced by the data user in ensuring compliance with the Act.

Many pharmacists tend towards the magpie approach to information in which almost anything is collected in case it comes in useful. The Fourth Data Protection Principle requires that the data held on computers should be scrutinised for adequacy and relevance and to ensure that they are not excessive for the purposes registered. The Registrar advises that the mere fact that certain information may be required in certain circumstances does not imply that this inforamtion should be routinely collected in all circumstances. Rather that the appropriate circumstances should be identified so that the information may be collected when it is required but not otherwise.

### 5.5.3  Recommendation

— Pharmacists should examine critically the personal data which they routinely collect bearing in mind that the mere assertion that certain information is relevant is not sufficient to comply with the Fourth Data Protection Principle; the assertion may need to be justified to the Registrar.

## 5.6  THE FIFTH PRINCIPLE

Personal data shall be accurate and, where necessary, kept up to date.

### 5.6.1  Explanation

Data are only considered inaccurate for the purpose of this principle if they are incorrect or misleading as to any matter of fact, as opposed to a question of opinion.

In the area of health care the requirement to keep data up to date can only be applied to those data classes relevant to the patient's personal life and circumstances.

### 5.6.2  Steps to Ensure Accuracy and Currency

A number of steps can be taken to help to ensure the accuracy of data and to provide a defence against claims by patients regarding inaccurate data. They include:

— checks on the accuracy of data provided by reference to original documentation, ie proper input checking procedures;

— checks built into the software to help ensure that data are validated on entry and comply with certain predetermined criteria; eg that the quality of medicine supplied is reasonable, 50 not 5000 tablets;

— the prompt investigation and correction of errors in data and faults in software;

— pharmacists giving patients the opportunity to check their records if they wish.

Where patients are seen on a regular basis, it is likely that the pharmacist will be aware of any changes, eg change of address, and update his records accordingly.

### 5.6.3  Recommendations

— To ensure that the original data are accurate, new patients may be invited to complete a questionnaire which will form the basis of the initial record.

— Operating procedures and software design should incorporate controls to ensure that only valid data are accepted and recorded on the correct record.

— Queries and complaints about inaccuracies should be handled quickly and sympathetically.

— Internal procedures should be specified which ensure that opportunities are taken to review and cross-check the personal data already held with the data subject either on a regular basis or when the opportunity arises.

— The software should provide an audit trail so that alterations to files can be monitored.

## 5.7  THE SIXTH PRINCIPLE

Personal data held for any purpose or purposes shall not be kept for longer than is necessary for that purpose or those purposes.

### 5.7.1  Explanation

Data which are held for historical, statistical or research purposes may be kept indefinitely, provided that the data are used in such a way that no damage or distress is, or is likely to be, caused to any patient.

Prudent computer housekeeping should dictate that data are kept for no longer than is necessary.

### 5.7.2  Data Retention

There are a number of legal requirements which apply to the retention of data relating to financial transactions and to the treatment and investigation of patients.

Where statutory limitation periods apply, these provide guidance on the appropriate periods for holding certain data. For example, financial data must be retained for at least six years for tax purposes and, in some instances, longer. Similarly the Consumer Protection Act requires data on drugs supplied to be retained for ten years. To answer any claims for personal injury it may even be necessary to retain patient care data for some time after a patient's death.

At the present time, the characteristics of computer systems are not well adapted to long term storage of personal data. Among the advantages of removing obsolete personal information from the computer systems are:

— reduction in the volume of information to be controlled;

— reduction in the cost of storage media;

— reduction in the administration of subject access.

Where there is no need for personal data to be held in a form that allows processing, consideration should be given to the possibility of using microfilm or microfiche output and erasing personal data from the computer system. This approach, where it is appropriate, has the attraction of being capable of giving operational access to the data without retaining it on the computer system. The use of microform media provides a very compact means of holding personal information and the microfilm, or microfiche, can readily be destroyed when it is no longer required. In either case, disclosures of the data continue to be controlled by the registration of the data usage.

### 5.7.3  Recommendations

— Pharmacists should develop and keep under review a policy, in conjunction with relevant advisers, on how long records will be held and in what detail in order to meet statutory claims, evidence in case of litigation, legitimate business needs and to support ongoing evidence in case of litigation.

— Deletions should be carried out at appropriate intervals to remove data that are no longer required. A proper archiving policy needs to be established. For example, an annual purge of redundant data should be performed.

### 5.8  THE SEVENTH PRINCIPLE

An individual shall be entitled:

a) at reasonable intervals and without undue delay or expense:

    i) to be informed by any data user whether he holds personal data of which that individual is the subject, and

    ii) to access any such data held by a data user; and

b) where appropriate, to have such data corrected or erased.

### 5.8.1 Explanation

The principle is interpreted by reference to section 21 of the Act and the Registrar's Guideline 5 which set out the rights of subject access in more detail.

### 5.8.2 Exempt Data

Personal data held for research purposes, P016, are exempt from subject access provided they are not used for any other purpose and that the resulting statistics or results of the research are not made available in a form which enables any patient to be identified.

### 5.8.3 Modified Access to Personal Health Information

An Order came into effect on 11 November 1987 which allows a pharmacist to withhold health data which are likely to cause serious harm to the physical or mental health of the patient. The Order does not absolve the pharmacist from the need to respond to a subject access request. It only allows him to withhold the specific harmful data. However, the Royal Pharmaceutical Society recommends its members to consult the relevant prescriber *before* providing subject access.

When in accordance with this Order a pharmacist decides not to supply all the data relevant to the patient, he is advised not to tell the patient that he is withholding information but to include the statement 'This is the data which I am required by law to provide' in his reply.

The Order also permits the pharmacist to withhold any data which would lead to the identification of another person unless that person is another health professional who has been involved in the care of the patient.

On those occasions when the data user is a company rather than a pharmacist, for example, large multiple chemists, the data user should not supply health care information without consulting the superintendent pharmacist or a pharmacist nominated by him.

The patient retains the right to apply to the Registrar if he believes data has been withheld. In considering the request, the Registrar will have the benefit of an appropriate professional.

### 5.8.4 Reasonable Intervals

Data may be accessed at reasonable intervals by the patient. What constitutes a 'reasonable interval' is clearly a matter of judgement but much may depend on the frequency with which the data are updated and their sensitivity.

A patient who continually requests subject access rights to his data when they are unlikely to have been changed is probably making unreasonable access requests. On the other hand, a patient who has made a valid complaint of inaccurate data being held, would not be making an unreasonable request in repeating his access rights in order to satisfy himself that action had been taken to have his data corrected or erased.

### 5.8.5 Data to be Provided

The Act leaves the onus to apply for subject access on the individual. Where the pharmacist has more than one registered entry the patient should state to which of these entries his request relates. In the interest of good relations, the patient should be offered guidance on the relevance of each register entry to enable him to select the appropriate ones for access.

Any coded information must be accompanied by a written explanation.

Where information about an individual is kept and it is not, nor intended to be, processed by reference to that individual, then it will not be personal data falling within the scope of the Act. However, the use of 'key-word' search software or some other means to pin-point data relating to an individual could make such data personal data falling within the scope of the Act.

The pharmacist must respond to a subject access request within 40 days of receiving it. This period does not start until he has, where necessary, received any information reasonably required to identify the patient or to locate the data.

## 5.8.6  Identification of the Enquirer

In order to prevent inadvertent disclosure to an unauthorised person, the identity of the enquirer should be established.

Subject requests should always be made in writing by the patient. One means of establishing the *bona fides* of an enquirer is to ask for information which can be checked from details in the patient's record.

## 5.8.7  Subject Access of Minors

In the context of health care data, it is worth quoting the guidance given by the Registrar on the subject of access rights of children or their parents:

> All individuals, including children, have the right of subject access. However, a child will not always be able to make his or her own request. The way in which the subject access right will work in this situation depends on the general law relating to the legal capacity of children. The law of Scotland differs in this respect from that of the rest of the United Kingdom.

> A data user in England, Wales and Northern Ireland who receives a subject access request from or on behalf of a child will need to judge whether the child understands the nature of the request.

> If the child does understand, he or she is entitled to exercise the right and the data user should reply to the child. A reply should be given to a request made on the child's behalf by a parent or guardian only if the data user is satisfied that the child has authorised the request.

> If the child does not understand, the parent or guardian is entitled to make the request on behalf of the child and to receive the reply. Parents or guardians should only make such a request in the interests of the child, not in their own interests.

> In Scotland, individuals under the age of 18 are, for legal purposes, either 'pupils' or 'minors'. Until the age of minority is reached (12 years for a girl and 14 for a boy) the child is a pupil. From that age until he or she reaches 18 the child is a minor.

> For a pupil the subject access right will be exercised by the person entitled under Scots law to act as the 'tutor' of the child —

this will usually be the parent.

Minors will be entitled to exercise the right for themselves. The data user is not required to obtain the consent of the parent or other tutor of the minor. A request by a minor's parent or tutor should only be complied with if there is evidence that the minor has authorised the request.

### 5.8.8  Identification of the Data Required

To establish the data required, the patient may be asked to provide the relevant identifier. He may also be asked for any additional information which may help to identify the data in which he is interested, eg dates, nature of the service provided. This will help to locate obscure records which are possibly registered separately from the main files.

### 5.8.9  Fees

A pharmacist is entitled to charge a fee, subject to a statutory maximum, for providing subject access. A separate fee is legally chargeable for access to each registered entry. At present (November 1989) the maximum fee chargeable is £10 per register entry.

### 5.8.10  Recommendations

— Procedures must be drawn up for handling subject access requests. These should specify the information required to help identify the individual and locate the data required, including archived data.

The procedures should be understood by all staff involved. It may be useful to draw up a standard request form. Details of the procedures should be made available to patients who may wish to access the data held about them but should not be so cumbersome as to deter enquiries.

— A mechanism should be provided to supply written explanations of any coded information.

— Whilst not a requirement of the Act, good pharmacist-patient relationships may best be served by arranging to deliver the response at a private consultation so that any technical terms can be explained.

— It may be desirable to ask the software supplier to incorporate a pro forma in the program package for use for subject access.

— When responding to a subject access request, the sensitivity of the data should be a factor in determining how much evidence of identity should be sought.

## 5.9  THE EIGHTH PRINCIPLE

Appropriate security measures shall be taken against unauthorised access to, or alteration, disclosure or destruction of personal data and against accidental loss or destruction of personal data.

### 5.9.1  Explanation

This principle applies to both data users and computer bureaux and is concerned with the issue of data security, encompassing the prevention of:

— unauthorised access to personal data either by physical entry to the premises or by logical access;

— the alteration, disclosure or destruction of data without the authority of the data user;

— the accidental loss or destruction of data because of human error, unreliable hardware, software or back-up and recovery procedures.

In interpreting the principle, particular consideration will be given to security needs in the light of the sensitivity of the data and the harm that could result from any of the events referred to by the principle. Attention will be paid to the physical security of the computer installation, to security measures programmed into the software and to the reliability of staff using data. Procedures for staff selection, induction and training in the use of the system may need to be provided.

### 5.9.2  Physical Security

The building housing a computer installation should be adequately protected against such contingencies as fire, flood and break-in.

If there are insufficient access controls on personal computers or terminals, the equipment should either be locked away when not in use or keyboard locks fitted.

If the dispensary where VDU screens are situated is visible to customers or the screens are visible from outside the building, they should be positioned so that they cannot be read by someone not authorised to do so.

When not in use, or during out-of-work hours, procedures must be followed for locking up tapes, disks and print-outs in a fireproof, secure place. Fireproof safes are available from computer-consumables suppliers.

### 5.9.3 Software Security

A range of factors needs to be considered including the following:

— thorough testing of the reliability and integrity of the software to ensure that it performs to its specification;

— in-built checks to validate the input of data;

— back-up and restore facilities to ensure the ability of the system to recover data;

— procedures requiring the duplication of data on a regular basis and their removal to a safe and secure place, eg to another site;

— thorough training of staff in the use of all relevant procedures relating to the system and their responsibilities for maintaining data privacy.

### 5.9.4 Data Access Controls

Factors to be considered include the following:

— the use of passwords, or other identifiers, to limit access to defined parts or levels of the system on a 'need to know' basis;

— clear policies and procedures regarding the issuing, changing and deletion of passwords and clearly laid down responsibilities for monitoring the effectiveness of these procedures;

— audit facilities to check who is accessing the system and for what purpose.

### 5.9.5 Disposal of Media

Unwanted and out-of-date print-outs containing personal data must be disposed of securely by shredding or incineration. This applies to hard-copy screen prints, any specialised documents and computer listings; they must never be re-used for scrap paper. Carbon paper and one-time printer ribbons must also be disposed of securely if they have been used in the production of personal data.

Where magnetic media are disposed of, any personal data must be completely overwritten by use of a special routine which is normally available from the supplier of the software. Use of a Delete command in the general software usually only removes the file or record name from the index and the data can still be retrieved by knowledgeable computer personnel.

### 5.9.6 Compensation for Loss or Unauthorised Disclosure

A claim for compensation can be made by a patient through the court against the pharmacist, or against a computer bureau, if he has suffered damage because there has been a breach of security on their part leading to the loss, destruction or unauthorised disclosure of his personal data.

However, no compensation is payable if the pharmacist or computer bureau can *prove* that all reasonable care was taken to prevent the loss, destruction or disclosure, or if the personal data are disclosed to or accessed by a person described in the disclosures section of the register entry relating to the data.

### 5.9.7 Recommendations

— Where data are particularly sensitive and are held by a computer bureau, this fact should be made known to the bureau and clearly specified in the contract between the parties.

— The physical security of the computing environment should be such as to reduce the opportunities of unauthorised access to the equipment and there should be adequate precautions against theft of either the computing equipment or its associated storage or output media, as well as fire, flood or other disasters.

— The logical security determines who shall have access to the programs and data. Its purpose is to reduce the opportunities for unauthorised access to, amendment or destruction of the personal data held. Pharmacists must satisfy themselves that the controls provided are effective.

— All copies of personal data either for input to the computer system or output, or obtained from the system, whether recorded on paper, microfilm or computer readable media, should be held secure from unauthorised access and securely destroyed or erased when they are no longer required.

— The practice of maintaining a cycle of three generations of back-up copies should ensure that it is possible to recover after system failure. Where the personal data are of a particularly sensitive, extensive, potentially damaging or distressing nature, back-up copies must be stored away from the premises.

# 6    Code of Practice for Property Management

## Note by Data Protection Registrar

*I welcome this valuable initiative taken by the National Computing Centre with support from the Department of Trade and Industry. I am pleased to note that the document has been developed in collaboration with the Royal Institute of Chartered Surveyors, the Incorporated Society of Valuers and Auctioneers, and the National Association of Estate Agents.*

*The guidance given will be useful in an area of activity where sensitive personal data may well be kept and at a time when many firms have only recently computerised their operations. It outlines practices which will assist them to comply with the data protection principles. The emphasis given to the practical application of the principles should prove particularly helpful.*

*Experience of data protection issues and of the practical application of the Act is developing rapidly. Data users should be aware, therefore, that the guidance given in this document is likely to need re-assessment from time to time.*

*I now look to data users to develop their own more detailed and specific procedures which will ensure that the data protection principles are met.*

## 6.1  INTRODUCTION

### 6.1.1  Purpose

This code relates to the use of computers by estate agents and property managers in the furtherance of their business objectives and is intended to assist them to comply with the Data Protection Act.

The Act requires users of computerised personal data, unless exempt, to register their data usage, to grant an individual access to his or her data and to abide by the eight data protection principles. This code explains the principles of the Act in the context of estate agency and property management. It is intended to help the data user to interpret the principles for his particular circumstances.

### 6.1.2  Scope

This code refers to property management data covered by the Data Protection Act, ie personal data recorded in a form in which they can be processed by equipment operating automatically, as defined in the Act, by or on behalf of a data user.

The definitions of the above terms are set out in section 1 of the Act, which should be consulted for clarification. Briefly, the Act is concerned only with computer-held data which relate to a living individual. The data subject is the individual referred to by the data. The data user is the organisation that controls the use and content of the data, whether it processes the data on its own equipment or makes use of another's processing facilities, ie a computer bureau. The term computer bureau refers to a person or organisation which provides data services to others, either by processing data for others by equipment operating automatically, as defined by the Act, or by allowing others to use equipment in its possession to carry out such processing. Processing is defined by the Act to mean amending, adding to, deleting or rearranging the data or extracting the information that contains the data.

### 6.1.3  Registered Purposes

This section sets out those of the Registrar's standard purposes which have been used to determine the area of activity addressed by this code.

Estate agents may be involved in some other activities as the result of being agents for a particular building society or insurance company. However, these purposes constitute ancillary activities in the context of estate agents and property managers and are not covered in this code.

In order to exercise their profession effectively, those working in the areas covered by this code often need to collect a great deal of personal and, in some instances, potentially sensitive information about their clients' circumstances. It is, therefore, appropriate for them to be particularly diligent in observing not only the letter but the spirit of the Act.

Good management practice, high standards of client administration or the desire for good customer relations may, on occasion, indicate a need to go beyond the actual requirements of the Act.

To simplify the registration process, the Registrar has devised a number of standard purposes. Those which are relevant in the context of this code are:

P020   Property Management

The management and administration of land and property.

P021   Housing Management

The administration and management of residential property.

P004   Marketing and Selling (Including Direct Marketing to Individuals)

The identification of potential customers and administration of promotional campaigns including selling or promotion to individuals by direct marketing methods.

### 6.1.4   Other Sources of Guidance and Information

The Act itself is the definitive statement of the law. The guidance provided in this code should be read subject to the provisions of the Act and any decisions of the Data Protection Tribunal and the higher courts.

This code is only intended to provide guidance to organisations and bodies in the particular area of property and housing management. Many data users may have other computerised activities. Readers are therefore advised to seek guidance on these other areas. Other sources of assistance include publications produced by the Registrar, the National Computing Centre and trade associations and representative bodies. The Bibliography lists a number of these publications.

Data users can also seek advice directly from the Registrar on how to comply with the Data Protection Act. Additionally they may find it helpful to refer queries on the Act to their trade association. A data user might also decide that it would be helpful to seek advice from their internal and/or external auditors on how to develop procedures to meet the requirements of the Act.

### 6.1.5 Breaches of the Act

Generally the requirements of the Act tie in closely with the aims of the good computer user who will wish to keep data secure and accurate, to limit disclosure to the right people and to keep the data subject informed.

Nevertheless, the Act does provide for sanctions against those who ignore its provisions. Failure to comply with an Enforcement Notice will be an offence and may lead to the imposition of fines, seizure of data and deregistration. Prosecution may also follow a failure to register or the use, collection, transfer or disclosure of data beyond the registered particulars.

Similarly, data users should bear in mind that data subjects, who suffer damage as a result of inaccurate data, loss of data, or unauthorised access to, destruction of or disclosure of data, may take legal action to seek recompense.

### 6.1.6 Summary

The Act requires users of computerised personal data, with very limited exemptions, to:

— collect and use personal data fairly;

— register the purposes for which they keep such data;

— use and disclose personal data only in accordance with the registration entry;

— ensure the relevance of the data kept and their accuracy and currency;

— delete obsolete data;

— respond to requests for copies of the data by the subject;

— protect the data.

### 6.1.7  Structure

In the remainder of this code the implications for estate agents and property managers of each data protection principle is examined in turn.

An explanation of the meaning of each principle is provided together with advice and recommendations to ensure compliance.

There is an obligation on all data users to observe all the principles set out in Schedule 1 of the Act and an obligation on computer bureaux to observe the Eighth Principle which relates to data security.

## 6.2  THE FIRST PRINCIPLE

The information to be contained in personal data shall be obtained, and personal data shall be processed, fairly and lawfully.

### 6.2.1  Explanation

Anyone providing information should not be deceived or misled as to the purpose for which the data will be used or disclosed. Information is always treated as having been fairly obtained when the person from whom the information was obtained was authorised or required by law to supply it.

Similarly, information disclosed by a person will always be treated as having been fairly obtained to the extent that the disclosure was required and authorised by law, even though the disclosure may not have been indicated to the data subject at the time the information was collected, eg information given to the police when required or authorised by statute will be fairly disclosed.

In determining whether information has been obtained fairly, the primary matters to be considered are the means by which the information was obtained and the understanding of the provider of the data as to the uses and disclosures that would be made of such data.

Data held for historical, statistical or research purposes and not used in a way which causes or is likely to cause damage or distress will not be regarded as having been obtained unfairly merely because these uses were not specified to the person providing the information.

### 6.2.2 Fair Obtaining and Processing of Personal Data

Data collected for the purposes of estate agency and property management should be obtained from reliable sources and only be used for that purpose. For example, the mailing list of past and current clients may not be sold to a firm of, say, fitted bedroom suppliers, unless a person providing his name and address has been told that this may happen at the time the information is obtained.

Unless the individual supplying the information can reasonably be expected to appreciate, without explanation, the purposes for which the data user intends to use, or disclose, the information, the data user should provide an explanation before the information is obtained.

Further information on this subject may be found in Guideline 4, obtainable from the Office of the Data Protection Registrar.

### 6.2.3 Recommendations

— Personal data collected by data users should be used only for legitimate business purposes.

— Where the data subject provides information by completing a form or entering details on a computer terminal, an explanation of the purposes for which the data are required should be provided.

### 6.3 THE SECOND PRINCIPLE

Personal data shall be held only for one or more specified and lawful purposes.

### 6.3.1 Explanation

This principle is complied with by registration provided that the data user only processes data in accordance with the purpose(s) registered.

### 6.3.2 Registered Purposes

Uses of data which might be expected to form part of property and housing management are given below and are derived from the Registrar's standard purpose descriptions referred to above at 6.1.3.

*P020 (Property Management)*

Typical activities which might be expected are:

— the preparation and maintenance of agreements, leases and rents;

— buying and selling property;

— checking the financial status of tenants and purchasers;

— keeping accounts;

— managing construction, installation, improvements, repair and maintenance;

— analysis for management and statutory returns.

Within these activities, the following functions may be carried out:

— recording and processing landlords' and tenants' instructions;

— controlling and monitoring the payment of rent and service charges;

— producing arrears lists and issuing reminders;

— recording the issue of notices in connection with rent reviews, lease expiries, property inspections;

— maintaining income and expenditure accounts on behalf of landlords;

— aggregating supplier accounts for work on different tenants' premises;

— dealing with complaints from landlords and tenants;

— production of taxation information for overseas clients;

— recording valuation information prior to receiving instructions;

— recording visits by prospective purchasers or tenants;

— progressing and monitoring sales;

— generating offers to landlords or tenants;

— maintaining negotiators' diaries.

*P021 (Housing Management)*

Typical activities include:

— the receipt and processing of applications;

— allocation of accommodation;

— rent accounting;

— keeping maintenance records;

— related legal and accounting matters;

— analysis for management purposes and statutory returns.

Within these activities, the following functions may be carried out:

— recording and processing vendors' and tenants' instructions;

— controlling and monitoring the payment of rent and service charges;

— producing arrears lists and issuing reminders;

— recording the issue of notices in connection with rent reviews, lease expiries, property inspections;

— maintaining income and expenditure accounts on behalf of landlords;

— dealing with complaints from landlords and tenants.

*P004 (Marketing and Selling, Including Direct Marketing to Individuals)*

Typical activities include:

— the classification, rating or checking of individuals;

— distribution of promotional materials by mail, door-to-door delivery or other means;

— telephone or face-to-face marketing or canvassing;

— dealing with complaints or enquiries;

— analysis for management purposes and statutory returns.

Within these activities the following functions may be carried out:

— recording and processing prospective purchasers' and tenants' requirements;

— recording mailings to prospective purchasers and tenants;

— recording visits to and by prospective purchasers and tenants;

— preparing lists of potential purchasers and tenants to secure instructions;

— sending mail shots to specific members of the public, eg offering free valuation;

— progressing mail campaigns;

— recording details of sales information despatched;

— recording telephone or face-to-face marketing or canvassing.

### 6.3.3 Exemption from the Act

Within the Act, exemption is provided in limited circumstances, for word processing and accounts processing. Guideline 6 describes the exemptions.

However, in practice, the constraints on what data may be held and what disclosures made in connection with these applications are such that registration of all processing is strongly recommended.

It is unlikely that property managers who use a computer in their business will be exempt from registering P020.

### 6.3.4 Recommendations

— Estate agents and property managers should normally register under Standard Purposes P020 and P004. The additional Purpose P021 must also be registered when applicable.

— Property managers must ensure that the processing of data about clients conforms to the registered particulars, including any processing of the data about clients by branch offices. They should also ensure that registered particulars are kept up to date or reviewed as usage changes.

## 6.4  THE THIRD PRINCIPLE

Personal data held for any purpose or purposes shall not be used or disclosed in any manner incompatible with that purpose or those purposes.

### 6.4.1  Explanation

This principle will be complied with provided that data are only used for the purpose(s) specified and disclosed only to those described in the data user's Register entry.

### 6.4.2  Disclosures of Personal Data

Reference by the Act to 'disclosing' data includes disclosing information extracted from the data. A disclosure occurs whenever the data, or information extracted from the data, are passed to someone other than the data user; whether this is done orally, in writing or by showing the other person a print-out or a screen on which the information is displayed.

With some exceptions (6.4.3 below), disclosures of personal data can only be made to the persons described in the disclosures section of the part of the data user's entry which relates to that data.

Other disclosures may result in an action for personal damages by a data subject against a data user.

If the data are to be transmitted overseas, the countries or territories involved must be named in the registered entry.

### 6.4.3  Exemptions

In certain circumstances, client data may be disclosed even though the disclosure has not been registered. Clients' data may always be disclosed:

— to the client, to the client's authorised agent or at the request of the client;

— to the employees or agents of the data user to enable them to perform their duties as employees or agents;

— for the purpose of obtaining legal advice, or in the course of legal proceedings in which the person making the disclosure is a party or a witness;

— for the prevention of injury or damage to health of anyone;

— for national security reasons;

— for the purposes of the assessment or collection of any tax or duty; the prevention or detection of crime; the apprehension or prosecution of offenders: but only where a denial of disclosure would be likely to prejudice one of those purposes;

— when required by statute, by any rule of law or by any order of the court.

When making disclosures under any of these exemptions, the data user must be satisfied that it is one which complies with the requirements of the particular non-disclosure exemption, eg where a disclosure is made to the police for a crime prevention purpose, it would be advisable to ensure that it is only done on the basis of a written statement provided by a senior police officer indicating that it is his belief that the disclosure falls within the terms of the exemption.

### 6.4.4  Recommendations

— Principals should lay down procedures and train their staff to ensure that the use and disclosure of personal data conform to the registered particulars.

— Managers should complete the Registrar's standard disclosure box D206, covering disclosure to suppliers, providers of goods or services. Inclusion of this disclosure covers those occasions when data may be inadvertently disclosed when a computer engineer is rectifying a machine or software malfunction.

— Firms with overseas offices to which they transfer data will need to complete the relevant section of the application for registration.

— Data users should adopt a clear policy on the confidentiality of all data relating to their clients.

### 6.5  THE FOURTH PRINCIPLE

Personal data held for any purpose or purposes shall be adequate, relevant and not excessive in relation to that purpose or those purposes.

### 6.5.1 Explanation

This principle is aimed at ensuring that the personal data held for a particular purpose are sufficient, but not more than sufficient, for that purpose. In order to comply with this principle, estate agents and property managers should review objectively what information is gathered about individuals and whether it is sufficient, relevant and not excessive, in each case, for property management or estate agency purposes.

## 6.5.2 Adequacy and Relevance

Data maintained in order to provide service to clients may include family and social circumstances, financial and transaction details and business information. No definitive list can be provided since the detail depends on the actual purpose for which the data are required. However, for data to be adequate and relevant they must seek to provide complete but not excessive information, all of which is likely to be used for property management purposes, eg Personal Habits (C013) or Lifestyle (C036) may be relevant to P020 (Property Management) since a landlord may wish to specify that his residence is only let to non-smokers or families without pets. It is unlikely that such information will be required in the case of purchasers.

Careful consideration should be given to avoiding the collection of information which cannot be fully justified. Information which is gathered just in case it might be useful might well breach this principle as being irrelevant or excessive for the purpose.

Computerised data may be supplemented by manual information, so this will be pertinent to any assessment of the adequacy of data.

## 6.5.3 Recommendation

— Principals should consider the data which are held in the light of the full range of client services provided and should be aware that they might be required to provide an objective explanation of why items of data are being held.

## 6.6 THE FIFTH PRINCIPLE

Personal data shall be accurate and, where necessary, kept up to date.

## 6.6.1 Explanation

Data are only considered inaccurate for the purpose of this principle if they are incorrect or misleading as to any matter of fact.

Updating is only required 'where necessary', so data held as an historical record of transactions is unlikely to be in need of updating but must be accurate at the time of entry. Recording the date of entry or update will assist any judgements made using the data.

Certain items of data will never change, for example, the date at which a tenancy started. Other items which are used to make current judgements need to be up to date. For example current salary information may need to be confirmed before a new lease is granted to a tenant.

### 6.6.2 Steps to Ensure Accuracy

Bearing in mind the sensitivity of the data and the harm that might result if they are incorrect, a number of steps can be taken to ensure their accuracy and to provide a defence against claims by clients regarding inaccurate data:

— wherever possible, the original documentation should be completed by the data subject;

— reasonable checks on the accuracy of data provided by reference to original documentation, ie proper input checking procedures;

— checks built into the software to help ensure that data are validated on entry and comply with certain predetermined criteria, eg checking that income values are within reasonable limits, matching payments received to the relevant rent request;

— the provision to clients of a formal acknowledgement of instructions received and the opportunity to raise queries, investigate them and correct the record where appropriate;

— the prompt investigation and correction of errors in data and faults in software.

### 6.6.3 Recommendations

— Property managers and estate agents should, wherever appropriate, seek to verify information obtained by reference to documentary evidence.

— Operating procedures and software design should incorporate controls to ensure that only valid data are accepted and are recorded on the correct record.

— Staff should deal quickly and sympathetically with client queries and complaints of inaccuracy.

— Vendors and landlords should be provided with acknowledgements of instructions.

— Prospective purchasers and tenants should be provided with a copy of their record and the opportunity to correct any inaccuracies.

## 6.7 THE SIXTH PRINCIPLE

Personal data held for any purpose or purposes shall not be kept for longer than is necessary for that purpose or those purposes.

### 6.7.1 Explanation

Data which are held for historical, statistical or research purposes may be kept indefinitely provided that the data are used in such a way that no damage or distress is, or is likely to be, caused to any data subject.

Data retained for other purposes should be subject to regular review and, when appropriate, deleted.

### 6.7.2 Present and Past Clients

Reasons for keeping data about present or past clients include acting on subsequent legal claims, the requirements of legislation (eg VAT) and audit.

Where statutory limitation periods apply, they provide guidance on the minimum periods for holding certain data, eg financial data must be retained for at least six years for tax purposes. Where they do not apply, judgements will need to be made about how long data should be held; holding data just in case it might be useful in the future is not permitted. There must be a specific period for reviewing data.

Good housekeeping practice suggests that data held, particularly on mailing lists, should be reviewed regularly to ensure that personal data are not held in breach of this principle. Data relating to the services provided to a purchaser or vendor are likely to be held at least for the current and previous trading years. In the case of landlords and tenants, a year after the expiration of the agreement may be appropriate. On occasions when data are retained for longer periods, the need to justify retention should be borne in mind.

In all cases, the length of time various classes of data should be held should be discussed with both the internal and external auditors.

### 6.7.3  Prospective Clients

Where data are collected concerning prospective clients, in advance of instructions being received and, subsequently the business does not materialise, the data should not be retained longer than might be considered reasonable for the purpose for which they were originally collected.

### 6.7.4  Recommendations

— Principals should develop and keep under review a policy, in conjunction with their organisation's internal and external auditors, on how long records will be held and in what detail in order to meet statutory claims or legitimate business needs.

— Deletions should be carried out at appropriate intervals to remove data that are no longer required.

— Even though the Act provides that data held for historical, statistical or research purposes may be kept indefinitely, it is good practice to depersonalise such data as early as possible.

### 6.8  THE SEVENTH PRINCIPLE

An individual shall be entitled:

a) at reasonable intervals and without undue delay or expense:

   i) to be informed by any data user whether he holds personal data of which that individual is the subject, and

   ii) to access to any such data held by a data user; and

b) where appropriate, to have such data corrected or erased.

### 6.8.1  Explanation

The principle should be interpreted by reference to section 21 of the Act. Section 21 is explained in some detail in the Registrar's Guideline 5. 'Reasonable' intervals between access requests will be interpreted in the light of the nature of the data, their purpose and the frequency with which they are updated. The correction or erasure of data is appropriate only where necessary to comply with other data protection principles.

### 6.8.2  Data to be Provided

All data, current and historical, held on an individual client, including both facts and opinions, such as credit worthiness, fall within the definition of personal data.

It should be noted that data coming under the overall description of client information may be held on more than one system within the organisation and may also include client data held by negotiators at branch offices on desk-top computers.

Where information about an individual is kept and it is not, nor intended to be, processed by reference to that individual, then it will not be personal data falling within the scope of the Act. However the use of 'key-word' search software or some other means to pin-point data relating to an individual would make such data personal data falling within the scope of the Act.

Access need not be provided to what the Act terms the 'intentions' of the data user. Intentions may include, for instance, specific leases to be granted or terminated or planned rent increases.

Where data to which access is being provided contains a reference identifying an individual other than the data subject, the data identifying that individual need not be disclosed unless the other individual has consented to the disclosure. However, the data user should still give as much information as possible to the data subject without revealing the identity of the other individual. This may involve editing the material to remove names or other identifying features.

Data held only for statistical purposes or research are exempt from the subject access provisions on the condition that the resulting statistics or the results of the research do not identify individuals, and that the data are not used or disclosed for any other purpose. If it is impractical to depersonalise the data the principals should establish policies to ensure that the identities are not revealed.

### 6.8.3  Requests in Writing

Data users are only required to respond to written requests and are entitled to request reasonable further information to help locate the required records such as relevant reference numbers, the branch dealt with, the address of the property or nature of services received.

If the data user has more than one register entry; the data subject should state to which of these his request relates. In the interest of good relations, the data subject should be offered guidance on the relevance of each register entry to enable him to select the appropriate ones for access.

A data user is entitled to charge a fee, subject to a statutory maximum, for providing subject access. At present (November 1989) the maximum fee is set at £10. A separate fee is legally chargeable for access to each registered entry.

### 6.8.4  Response

The data user must respond to a subject access request within 40 days of receiving it. This period does not start until the data user has, where necessary, received any information reasonably required to identify the data subject or to locate the data.

During the time between receiving the request and replying to it, any normal amendments, or deletions may be made to the data. However, no special changes should be made simply because the request has been received. The data should be provided to the individual in written form and should be intelligible. Any coded information should be fully explained.

### 6.8.5  Identification of the Enquirer

In order to prevent inadvertent disclosure to an unauthorised person, the identity of the enquirer should be established. One means of establishing the *bona fides* of the enquiry is to ask for information which can be checked against details in the data subject's record.

### 6.8.6  Identification of the Data Required

To establish the data required, the enquirer should be asked to quote an appropriate reference. This could be a file number or the date on which the property was accepted by the data user. In many cases the name of the property owner will be sufficient.

Enquirers should be asked for any additional information which may help to identify the data in which they are interested. This will help to locate the less obvious records that may be held on micros and personal computers.

A data user is entitled to ask for information which he reasonably requires to locate the data requested. He may ask for additional information, which would be helpful though not reasonably required. He should make it clear that the data subject does not need to supply those extra details.

### 6.8.7 Manual Information

Manually held information lies outside the scope of the Act and this code. However, from time to time, requests may be received for access to manual data. It is suggested that organisations should look upon such requests favourably and provide access where it is practical and realistic to do so.

### 6.8.8 Recommendations

— Procedures must be drawn up for handling subject access requests. These should specify the information needed to help identify the individual and locate the data required. The procedures should be understood by all staff involved. It may be useful to draw up a standard request form. The procedures should be made available to clients who may wish to access the data held about them but should not be so cumbersome as to deter enquirers.

— When responding to a subject access request, the sensitivity of the data is a factor to be considered in determining how much evidence of identity should be sought.

### 6.9 THE EIGHTH PRINCIPLE

Appropriate security measures shall be taken against unauthorised access to, or alteration, disclosure or destruction of personal data and against accidental loss or destruction of personal data.

### 6.9.1 Explanation

This principle applies to both data users and computer bureaux and is concerned with the issue of data security, encompassing prevention of:

— unauthorised access to personal data either by physical entry to premises or by logical access;

— the disclosure or destruction of data without the authority of the data user;

— the accidental loss or destruction of data because of human error, unreliable hardware, software or back-up and recovery procedures.

In interpreting the principle, consideration should be given to security needs in the light of the sensitivity of the data and the harm that could result from any of the events referred to by the principle. Attention should be paid to the physical security of the computer installation, to security measures programmed into the software and to the reliability of staff using data. Procedures for staff selection, induction and training in the use of the system may need to be provided.

### 6.9.2  Physical Security

The building housing a mainframe computer installation should be adequately protected against such contingencies as fire, flood and break-in. Access to the installation should involve adequate security procedures, such as the use of badges, passes or electronic card systems, to reduce the likelihood of unauthorised access.

If there are insufficient access controls on personal computers or terminals, the equipment should either be locked away when not in use or keyboard locks fitted.

Where VDU screens are situated in places visited by members of the public, or are visible from outside the building, they should be positioned so that they cannot be read by someone not authorised to do so.

When not in use, or during out-of-work hours, procedures must be followed for locking up tapes, disks and print-outs in a fireproof, secure place.

### 6.9.3  Software Security

A range of factors needs to be considered including the following:

— thorough testing of the reliability and integrity of the software to ensure that it performs to its specification;

— in-built checks to validate the input of data;

— back-up and restore facilities to ensure the ability of the system to recover data;

— procedures requiring the duplication of data on a regular basis and their removal to a safe and secure place, eg to another site;

— thorough training of staff in the use of all relevant procedures relating to the system and their responsibilities for maintaining data privacy.

### 6.9.4 Data Access Controls

Factors to be considered include the following:

— the use of passwords, or other identifiers, to limit access to defined parts or levels of the system on a 'need to know' basis;

— clear policies and procedures regarding the issuing, changing and deletion of passwords and clearly laid down responsibilities for monitoring the effectiveness of these procedures;

— audit facilities to check who is accessing the system and for what purpose;

— the provision of security features within the operating software and the particular characteristics of the terminals in use.

### 6.9.5 Disposal of Media

Unwanted and out-of-date print-outs containing personal data must be disposed of securely by shredding or incineration. This applies to hard-copy screen prints, any specialised documents and computer listings; they must never be re-used for scrap paper. Carbon paper and one-time printer ribbons must also be disposed of securely if they have been used in the production of personal data.

Where outside contractors are employed to remove stationery waste, there must be proper contractual arrangements for the secure disposal of that relating to personal data and the data user must satisfy himself that they are being complied with.

Where magnetic media are disposed of, any personal data must be completely overwritten; the deletion of the file or record index is not sufficient.

### 6.9.6 Compensation for Loss or Unauthorised Disclosure

A claim for compensation can be made by a data subject to a court against a data user, or a computer bureau, which is involved in the processing of personal data which relates to him, if as a result of loss, or unauthorised access to, or unauthorised destruction or disclosure of his data, he has suffered damage.

However, no compensation is payable if the data user or computer bureau can prove that all such care was taken as was reasonably required to prevent the loss, access, destruction or disclosure.

### 6.9.7 Recommendations

— The requirements of the Data Protection Act must be included in an organisation's security policy, with special attention being paid to the secure storage and disposal of all types of computer printouts, hard copies of visual displays and magnetic media.

— Where data are particularly sensitive and are held by a computer bureau, this fact should be made known to the bureau and clearly specified in the contract between the parties. The bureau should also be provided with a list of disclosures which the data user gives its authority to make.

— The physical security of the computing environment should be such as to reduce the opportunities of unauthorised access to the equipment and there should be adequate precautions against theft of either the computing equipment or its associated storage or output media, as well as fire, flood or other disasters.

— The logical security should be such as to reduce the opportunities for unauthorised access to, amendment or destruction of, the personal data held.

— All copies of personal data either for input to the computer system or output, or obtained from the system, whether recorded on paper, microfilm or computer readable media, should be held secure from unauthorised access and securely destroyed or erased when they are no longer required.

— All personal data should be secured by adequate back-up copies to allow recovery from system failure. Where the personal data are of a particularly sensitive, extensive, potentially damaging or distressing nature, off-site storage of back-up copies should be considered to cope with extensive damage to the facilities at the location of the system.

— Information about an employee's responsibility for complying with the Act should be included in the contract of employment of any staff whose job provides access to personal data. Details of any disciplinary sanctions which will be applied, should he fail to comply, should also be provided.

— Where a computer bureau is used for processing, it should be provided with a list of disclosures which the data user authorises it to make.

# 7 Conclusion

The Data Protection Act itself is the only definitive statement of the law on data protection. The guidance provided in these codes should be read subject to the provisions of the Act and any decisions of the Data Protection Tribunal and courts of law.

The codes are only intended to provide guidance in the particular areas addressed. Many data users have other activities requiring the use of information technology. Readers are therefore advised to read and follow any other codes of practice devised by appropriate trade associations.

Data users and computer bureaux may seek advice directly from the Data Protection Registrar as to how to comply with the legislation. Additionally they may find it helpful to refer queries to their trade associations. A data user should also consider seeking advice from internal or external auditors on developing procedures to ensure compliance with the Data Protection Act.

The above codes of practice do not constitute a legal opinion. Although compliance with any code may be evidence of good practice, it will not guarantee immunity from the sanctions of the Act. Neither will failure to comply with a code constitute in itself a breach of the Act.

# Appendix

## Useful Addresses

1. The Office of the Data Protection Registrar
   Springfield House
   Water Lane
   Wilmslow
   Cheshire
   SK9 5AX
   Telephone: 0625 535777

2. National Computing Centre Limited
   Oxford Road
   Manchester
   M1 7ED
   Telephone: 061-228 6333

3. The British Computer Society
   13 Mansfield Street
   London
   W1M 0BP
   Telephone: 01-637 0471

4. Computing Services Association Limited
   Hanover House
   73/74 High Holborn
   London
   WC1V 6LE
   Telephone: 01-405 2171

5. The Confederation of British Industry
   Centre Point
   103 New Oxford Street
   London
   WC1A 1DU
   Telephone: 01-379 7400

6. The Chartered Institute of Management Accountants
   63 Portland Place
   London
   W1N 4AB
   Telephone: 01-637 2311

7. The Institute of Internal Auditors, United Kingdom
   82z Portland Place
   London
   W1N 3DH
   Telephone: 01-580 0101

8. The Institute of Personnel Management
   IPM House
   Camp Road
   Wimbledon
   London
   SW19 4UW
   Telephone: 01-946 9100

9. The Institute of Purchasing and Supply
   Easton House
   Easton on the Hill
   Stamford
   Lincolnshire
   PE9 3NZ
   Telephone: 0780 56777

10. The Incorporated Society of Valuers and Auctioneers
    3 Cadogan Gate
    London
    SW1X 0AS
    Telephone: 01-235 2282

11. The National Association of Estate Agents
    Arbon House
    21 Jury Street
    Warwick
    CV34 4EH
    Telephone: 0926 400953

12. The Royal Institute of Chartered Surveyors
    12 Great George Street
    Parliament Square
    London
    SW1P 3AD
    Telephone: 01-222 7000

13. The Royal Pharmaceutical Society of Great Britain
    1 Lambeth High Street
    London
    SE1 7JN
    Telephone: 01-735 9141

# Bibliography

### 1. HMSO:

*Data Protection Act 1984*                    ISBN 0 10 543584 8

### 2. Data Protection Registrar:

Guidelines to inform individuals of their rights under the Act and to help those who process personal data to understand their obligations.

| | |
|---|---|
| 1. *Introduction to the Act* | ISBN 1 870466 09 8 |
| 2. *The Definitions* | ISBN 1 870466 15 2 |
| 3. *The Register and Registration* | ISBN 1 870466 10 1 |
| 4. *The Data Protection Principles* | ISBN 1 870466 11 X |
| 5. *Individuals Rights* | ISBN 1 870466 12 8 |
| 6. *The Exemptions* | ISBN 1 870466 13 6 |
| 7. *Enforcement and Appeals* | ISBN 1 870466 14 4 |
| 8. *Summary for Computer Bureaux* | ISBN 1 870466 16 0 |

### 3. NCC:

*Data Protection Act Resource Pack*

— Lecture Notes, Student Notes, Visuals and Staff Notices intended for use by organisations to instruct their staff in the implications of the Act.

Elbra R A, *Guide to the Data Protection Act,* NCC Publications, 1984

— A short introduction to the Data Protection Act 1984. Describes

the circumstances under which organisations must register.
ISBN 0 85012 475 1

Hook Chris, *Data Protection Implications for Systems Design*, NCC Publications, 1989

— Gives practical guidance to system designers about the interpretation and implementation of data protection principles.
ISBN 0 85012 735 1

## 4. Institute of Personnel Management:

Evans Alastair, *The Data Protection Act: A Guide for Personnel Managers*, 1984

Evans Alastair, ed, *Data Protection Policies and Practice,* 1986

## 5. Department of Health:

Health Circular HC(87)14, September 1987, *Data Protection Act 1984: Modified Access to Personal Health Information*

Health Circular HC(87)26, November 1987, *Data Protection Act 1984: Modified Access to Personal Health Information*

*NHS Data Protection Handbook,* 1987

## 6. Institute of Chartered Accountants in England and Wales:

*Accounts Digest No. 205*, Business Documents — Management & Retention

— Sets out statutory retention periods for financial data.

*Information Technology Statement No. 3*, Control and Management of Information, 1987

— Deals with the control principles and procedures relating to data maintained on computer files and to the management of information derived from that data.
ISBN 0 85291 858 5